Designing Small Craft

Designing Small Craft

John Teale

First published 1976 in Great Britain by
Nautical Publishing Company
Lymington, Hampshire SO4 9BA

in association with
George G. Harrap & Company Limited
182–184 High Holborn, London WC1V 7AX

ISBN 0 245 52987 X

By the same author

- Fast Boats
- Care and Maintenance of Small Craft
- Small Craft Design and Construction
- Buying a Boat
- High Speed Motor Boats

Filmset and printed in Great Britain by
BAS Printers Limited, Wallop, Hampshire

CONTENTS

Introduction

The first thing anyone does when sketching out the profile of a new boat is to draw a straight line, representing the waterline, and then aportion some of the yacht above it and some below it. But at this point most people stick for they are convinced that some form of black magic must be invoked for the resulting completed vessel to retain these proportions. In fact this is one of the simplest bits of yacht designing because the whole thing can be worked out initially from a rough approximation formula and then, as a check, by a bit of straightforward mathematics. There is no intuition, experience or devilish cunning required though someone who had designed many craft before would generally find that the depth of boat below the waterline he had so airily drawn would turn out to be pretty near right when checked, while a first-timer might not be so lucky and would have to alter things a little. This initial step is the one that worries a professional designer least and since he is a normal human being, it should worry you least also.

If, then, that is not quite such a hurdle as was imagined it might follow that there is nothing desperately difficult about any aspect of boat design. To do the job properly takes time and your first effort is unlikely to prove to be the backbone of the Admiral's Cup team nor to win the Cowes–Torquay power boat race but it should certainly float at its designed waterline and do all sorts of unambitious things in a perfectly satisfactory manner.

In this book are a number of lines plans and constructional details of different types of boat for you to ponder. Included also are some general recommendations on more esoteric matters such as the best positions for the centres of buoyancy and effort. These may be of assistance in producing a boat with a respectable performance, but in any case study every published drawing and bit of technical information that may appear in any of the yachting journals and make notes of those that apply to the craft you are designing. Successful designing in the early stages is largely a matter of incorporating other people's ideas and recommendations into your own work. There's nothing to be ashamed of in that, everyone starts the same way.

May I make a plea that whether you are a sailing or power boat man that you sink your prejudices and look at all the plans in the book and read the text that goes with them? It is impossible to put sail and power into different compartments, for the general principles are the same for both and as the plot unfolds in successive pages and more detailed aspects of design are considered these may be explained in relation to either type. In any case antagonism between the two sorts of boating is ridiculous from a design standpoint. There can be just as much to designing a motor boat as a sailing craft and vice versa.

In a book like this what to leave out is just as difficult a decision as what to put in. So there are omissions. For instance, I have made only a brief mention of spars and none at all that I can recall of rigging. These are specialised fields where a little knowledge does not help very much. It is better to go and have a look at what has been done on similar boats or simply to trot cap in hand to an expert. The spar-building companies, for instance, would rather make a few recommendations than have their work collapse in a heap or fall over the side. Additionally, there are plenty of professional riggers about who will help.

Stability and its associated subject of power to carry sail are also ignored mainly because calculating the metacentric height is a tedious occupation and for the vast majority of craft a waste of time. Provided your dream boat has no extreme proportions and an eye is kept on published examples there should be few problems in that area.

On the construction side, ferro-cement has not been covered though typical weights for various lengths of hull are given in the table of weights and measures. Since ferro-cement craft do not usually have any framing other than that integral with the hull the figures given are simply multiplied by the superficial area of the hull (plus deck and upperworks if they, too, are of ferro) to give the light displacement.

Considering this book declares itself to be about design there may appear to be rather a lot on construction but it is not really possible to do a hull design without knowing how it is to be made. Constructional material affects the weight, of course, but also has a considerable bearing on the general shape of the hull. Unless designing for a production line it would not be too sensible, for instance, to plump for G.R.P. on a chine boat as that material has little inherent stiffness when compared with ply or steel and would need a deal of framing. Conversely, it is good for round bilge boats since the curves of that form build in stiffness. G.R.P. craft cannot come to a point at the bow or along the keel since it would be impossible to lay up the material and work the resin into a point. Radii are required, yet a frameless steel vessel shows a nearly knife-edge in these areas. That will all be explained a bit more fully in the book and I have only mentioned it here to illustrate that one would not normally design a boat without knowing the building material or how it was to be put together.

Finally, as it has been decreed that we should all hurry down the slope to a meaningless world conformity, I suppose measurements, weights and so forth should have been stated exclusively in metric units. But it seems that most people, including the younger generation, still think largely in Imperial units so I have stuck with those in the main though metric equivalents are given in most cases. Anyhow, I am not greatly enamoured with what we are assured is the more logical system. After some seven months' full-time exposure to metres, kilos and all the rest when working in Sweden I returned with some relief to a system where feet, inches, pounds and tons are all entirely separate things and whose nomenclature is not at the whim of some rashly placed decimal point. However, I suppose that prejudice is an indication of failing mental powers and I had probably better desist before condemning myself still further!

Three or four of the drawings in the book have appeared in *Motor Boat and Yachting.* The graphs showing G.R.P. thickness, stiffener spacing and equivalent strengths of sandwich material came from FRP Design Data published by Fibreglass Ltd. I am indebted to both for permission to reproduce the material.

Well, that's about it. I trust the book is reasonably enjoyable and makes sufficient sense for you to have a go at designing a boat and then, hopefully, to translate the pictures into reality by building the thing.

Four basic curves used in design drawing

1. Flat-Bottomed Boats

People tend to think of flat-bottomed craft as poor relations to 'proper' boats and in a way I suppose they are right. Given that money was no object there would be little point in building these very simple forms for they suffer from various disadvantages; the main one is a tendency to pound, particularly in short, steep seas; then because they must be long, low, lean and light to be successful sailers, the accommodation is bound to be somewhat restricted. Still, I have built four flatties of various sizes

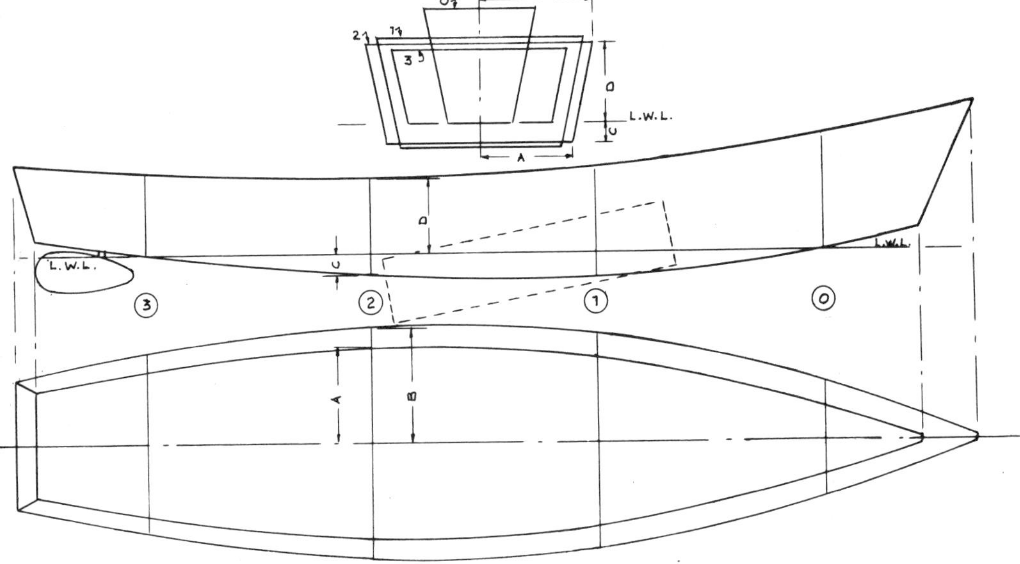

Fig 1 The configuration of a traditional sailing flattie with bow and stern well clear of the water and balanced rudder. The letters A to D all refer to station 2 and show what dimensions must correspond

and descriptions over the years and have been pleased with them all because they allow nearly instant boatbuilding and their final performance in each case has been a pleasant surprise.

Of course there have been flat-bottomed boats for centuries all over the world but the types we see in the West can be traced back to the Connecticut coast of the U.S.A. and from about 1835. They are reputed to have been developed by the oyster men of that region to replace log canoes when the supplies of large trees became a problem. Several forms of flatties evolved but nearly all had the same basic features of well rockered keels, flaring sides and length to beam ratio of four or five to one. Most had both bow and stern lifted clear of the water, as in fig 1, but one famous flattie, 'Nonpareil', was designed with her stem extending down just below the waterline. The object of this was to reduce pounding. Because of the small hull draught large centreboards were installed and rudders were balanced so that about one-third the area was ahead of the rudder stock—again as sketched in fig 1.

On boats of any size, a sort of ketch rig was usual with leg-of-mutton sails set on light, bendy spars. The foremast, placed very far forward, was about six times the beam in height and the mizzen only slightly shorter at around $5\frac{1}{2}$ beams in height.

In skilled hands the sharpie was considered fast and weatherly, but like so many of these locally-developed types a breed of sailors developed with them who were accustomed to their ways and idiosyncracies. For them the boats were safe.

If we are going to build a flattie today we can't do better than stick to the general form that has been handed down to us. A wide, flat-bottomed sailing boat is usually a disaster because though centreboards and rudders stuck deep into the water both help, nothing can replace the area of immersed hull as a deterrent to drifting to leeward under sail. The wider you make a flat-bottomed boat without increasing weight at a staggering rate, the less boat there will be in the water. So, a flattie must be kept narrow and even so will not have much in the way of hull draught. For that reason the topsides and cabins must be kept low or the windage will be too great and again you will be reduced to skittering sideways across the water. There was once a saying that the amount of boat above water should not be greater than the depth below. Thus you could have 4 ft overall freeboard if you had 4 ft hull draught and so on. Though nobody would seriously advance that as a fundamental design precept today, in general terms it still holds good.

Obviously one advantage of the flattie is that with lifting rudders and centreboards she is the last word in shoal draught yachts but in achieving this enviable status something has been lost as far as stability is concerned. The boat will need to be sailed carefully and with more attention than might be needed by her heftier rivals. Naturally ballast can be added. Inside ballast will not be very effective on such a shallow boat and the best answer, if shoal draught is not a requirement, would be to use a steel plate keel with a suitably-shaped iron or steel bulb at the bottom. With this arrangement a flattie could be made into quite a good offshore cruising boat. But do not elaborate too much or you will find that you could have built a better all-rounder for no more money and at the same speed.

Drawing Equipment

A flattie is the simplest of all types to design mainly because calculations for displacement and so forth can be done easily enough without a planimeter. Further, there are no tight curves which the first-time designer may find it tedious to fair. So, what do we need? Here is a list:

Pencil. I use a clutch pencil and an HB lead for all drawing work. Harder leads may draw finer lines but they make rubbing out, and there is plenty of that in design work, a mite difficult. Thus we also require:

Rubber. Buy a good, soft one and a . . .

Sharpener. If a clutch pencil is being used the sharpener will have to deal with leads only, not the whole pencil. Such things can be bought at drawing office supply shops but failing that a piece of sandpaper will suffice.

Set Squares. Two will be needed. One a biggish affair, say 18 in. (0.5 m) long on its longest edge, and another smaller square. It doesn't matter whether they are 45 degree or 30, 60, 90 degree squares.

Straight Edge. This is what it implies—a length of wood, Perspex or steel with one absolutely straight edge which should be at least 3 ft 6 in. (1 m) long.

Scale Rule. What you buy here depends on whether you are going for metric or Imperial units of length. Whichever is chosen select a rule that has as many different scales on it as possible. If you choose to carry on with Imperial measurements make sure the sub-divisions on the rules are in $\frac{1}{12}$ths, not $\frac{1}{10}$ths, because a twelfth of a foot is one inch and dimensions can then be read off in feet, inches and fractions of an inch.

Curves. Four basic ship curves are sketched and something like these should be bought. As time goes on and you become more ambitious other shapes can be added to your collection. Drawing office supply shops sell, or can get, these curves. The long ones are about 2 ft (0.6 m) in length, and all are used to draw curves too tight for a batten (q.v.).

Compasses. It is useful to have a pair of compasses for drawing transom and stem radii, ports and so on. Small affairs are usually spring bows which are more likely to draw circles without changing the radius half-way round, but have a look at a selection and see what you can afford. You must be able to draw big radii as well as small ones.

Batten and Weights. For the long curves on a boat, such as waterlines in plan view, the sheer line and probably the keel line, the greater part of most buttocks, diagonals and the like, a batten is a must. This is a long length of a flexible wood or Perspex (the latter is generally better) which is held in place with weights. There are all sorts of battens (sometimes called splines) made but the most generally useful is one about 4 ft long tapering from something like $\frac{1}{4}$ in. by $\frac{1}{8}$ in. at one end to $\frac{1}{4}$ in. by $\frac{1}{16}$ in. at the other. Metrically, that is something like 1.2 metres long and 6 mm by 4 mm tapering to 6 mm by 1 mm. The idea of the taper is that the more flexible end is used where the curve is tight. A batten can be used flat or on edge and six weights each about 4 lb (1.8 kilos) will suffice.

Drawing Board. That should about do but you will note that no drawing board has been mentioned. These are very expensive things in the fairly large sizes that are needed for yacht design work. Anything under 3 ft 6 in. by 2 ft 6 in. (1000 mm by 800 mm) is not much use and to begin with an ordinary table can be used with several thicknesses of paper under your drawing or tracing paper. The top of the table should be about 3 ft 4 in. high.

Paper. Most designing is done on tracing paper but when working on the lines plan you will have to use drawing paper for the tracing stuff expands and contracts with the weather so much that really accurate work is difficult. To fasten paper down masking tape at the corners is best. It can be peeled off without damage.

Drawing

Having assembled this selection of gear the time has come to make a start on the actual drawing. First of all sketch the boat freehand but to a definite scale to get an idea of what you want. If you go carefully and ply the rubber selectively a freehand drawing can be astonishingly accurate and even long curves will need little subsequent alteration. When the general outline of the boat and sail plan pleases you, sit back and admire it before doing the whole thing again! This time the job must be done accurately with the full panoply of drawing instruments. First draw a grid, fig 2, and make it as large as you conveniently can. When completed, scale up the previous drawing and put it in with curves, battens and so forth as carefully and accurately as possible.

Grid. The top horizontal line is the load waterline (LWL) in profile—that is the waterline at which the boat floats, you hope. The horizontal below it is the centreline of the boat in plan view; that is when viewed from above. Those two lines should be at a reasonable distance apart—reason being dictated by the proposed draught (excluding centreboards, rudders and so on) and the proposed half-beam of the vessel. So if you

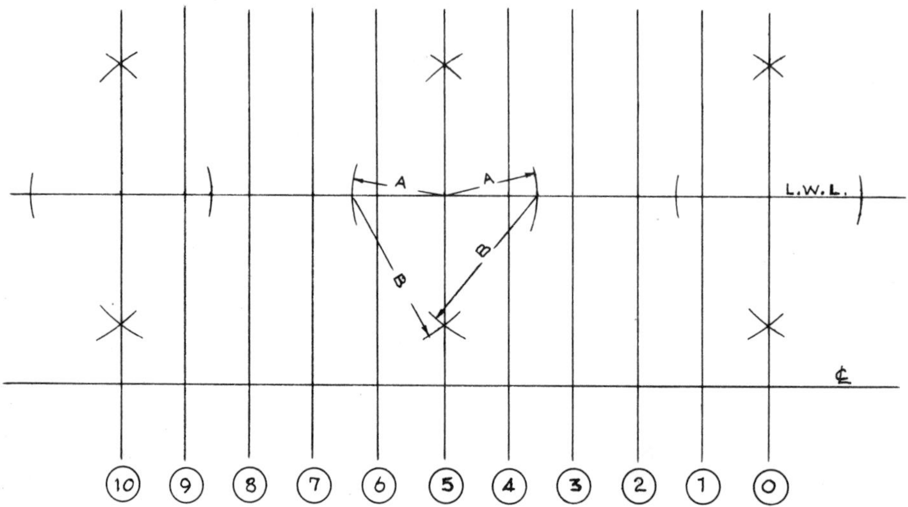

Fig 2 The grid that must be drawn accurately before starting off on the lines plan. Dimensions from your initial sketch, probably scaled-up, are transferred to this plan

were going to do this plan at, say 1 in. = 1 ft and the draught was to be 2 ft and the half beam 6 ft the two lines ought to be separated by 2 + 6 + a little bit; something like 9 in. would do, then. Next divide the load waterline into a definite number of equal parts whose total equals the waterline length of the boat. Almost any number will do, as will be demonstrated as we trudge along, but eight or ten are handy. Ensure that your spacings are really accurate, checking each and then the total. Then you must put vertical lines through all these spots which will eventually mark the various sections, or stations. Take three of them, as shown on fig 2 again, and with compasses draw arcs right and left. From the intersection of these arcs with the LWL draw further and bigger arcs above and below, then join up the intersections of these latter arcs through whatever station you are working on. These new lines should now be vertical. Measure down them and check that the plan centreline (CL) is really parallel to the LWL. Now on CL mark out the stations as you had them above. There will be three points already there but check, double check and alter as necessary. If you have a drawing pen, ink in the LWL, CL and station lines: if not, draw them in with a hard lead—something like a 3H.

This has probably been a tedious occupation conducive to stomach cramps and one question has been left in the air—what is the likely draught of the boat? We can now occupy ourselves with the first bit of mathematics required and couple this with a glance at the caption of fig 4. On this you will see that it is stated that the block coefficient is 0.57 ($C_B = 0.57$).

Block Coefficient

Technically this is the ratio of the immersed volume of the hull to the product of length, breadth and draught; that is, to the circumscribing block. Having said that let us do a couple of sums. That caption of fig 4 also gives waterline length, waterline beam and draught as 22 ft 8 in. (6.9 m); 4 ft 10 in. (1.47 m); and 8¼ in. (0.21 m) respectively. The displacement, or all-up weight, of the boat is also given as 1.2 tons (1220 kilos).

Now Block Coefficient or $C_B = \dfrac{\text{Disp.} \times 35}{L \times B \times D}$

where L is waterline length, B is waterline beam at 'midships, and D is draught at 'midships.

So in this case:

$$C_B = \frac{1.2 \times 35}{22.66 \times 4.8 \times 0.68} = 0.57$$

In that sum, feet and inches have been converted to feet and decimals of a foot. The formula can be twiddled round so that we can find the answer for draught, thus:

$$D = \frac{\text{Disp.} \times 35}{C_B \times L \times B}$$

Disp. is displacement in tons and multiplying by 35 gives tons in cubic feet volume of sea water, which is what we want. If the displacement of the boat had been worked out in pounds, then dividing that figure by 64 would also give a volume in cubic feet. If the displacement had been in kilogrammes shifting the decimal back three places gives the same thing in cubic metres. Thus 1220 kilos = 1.220 cubic metres. Going back to that fig 4 boat we can now do the sum, assuming that we know weight, length, breadth and block coefficient but not draught.

$$D = \frac{1.2 \times 35 \text{ (or 2690/64 if you had worked in pounds)}}{0.57 \times 22.66 \times 4.8} = 0.68 \text{ ft}$$

The sum is exactly the same in metrics and gives the same answer:

$$D = \frac{1.22}{0.57 \times 6.9 \times 1.47} = 0.21 \text{ metres}$$

Block coefficient is different for every boat but on each example given in this book a block coefficient is shown and this should provide a guide for any similar craft you draw. Of course you must have an idea of the weight of the craft but this can be worked out roughly. Table 1 shows the calculations for that 29-footer of fig 4. Be generous with your weight estimates. Nearly every boat turns out heavier than anticipated and anyway it is better to find the vessel floating a bit light rather than having her gunwale just breaking the water.

As can be seen, the total came to a little under a ton, but I then lost my nerve and added a bit more, making it 1.2 tons. At the end of this book is a table of weights that might help.

Preliminary Lines

Now you can draw with a bit of confidence and we will return to fig 1 which purports to show what points on a lines plan must agree with one another. Only four stations are shown, including station 0, and all letters and lines apply to station 2. It will be seen, I hope, that the width of the deck in plan view and sectional view (letters B) must be the same; the height of the deck in profile and section (letters D) must be the same; the width of the bottom (letters A) must agree on both views and the depth of the bottom below LWL (letters C) must correspond in profile and section. To check that distances are the same it is easier to make tick marks on a piece of paper and then offer the paper up to the view you are working on rather than make holes all over the place with dividers or try and measure things on a rule.

Note also that the deck and bottom endings must be in the same vertical line on both plan and profile views, at bow and stern.

Rabbet. Back to fig 3; sorry to keep dodging about like this but there seems to be no happy alternative. A mysterious word, Rabbet, has appeared and deserves a bit of explanation. Normally lines plans are drawn to the outside of planking and so, if you think about it, neither the deck nor the bottom can come to a point if only because there is the thickness of the planking to consider. But, in fact, that planking must land up on some structural member and such a member has a width of its own. If then, you had decided that the stem, and the stern post if you were designing a double ender, were to be 2 in. wide and the planking were to be let into it flush (glance at the bottom right hand sketch of fig 6 if this argument is tending to lose you) then the planking would end one inch off the centreline each side. So the width of the rabbet line would be 1 in. off CL.

Displacement

While perusing the lines plan of that 29 ft flattie note that only one side of the boat is drawn in plan view, with the same applying to the sections. Though fig 1 showed both sides it is a waste of effort to repeat that on a proper lines plan and also tends to confuse the issue. So, if we turn our attention to working out the displacement now, for which the areas of each section or station below LWL are needed, you will realise that measuring areas off a lines plan in fact gives half-areas. This is fine and what we want, so don't go multiplying by two. Instead, get the answers in square feet or square metres, jot down the figures, and turn to table 2. The lines plan of fig 3 had eight subdivisions and table 2 is set out accordingly. If yours had a different number table 4 shows a ten subdivision scheme, and table 6 a method for any odd number. What we want to do now is check that having drawn the lines plan the draught is as you had planned and that the boat will float at its intended waterline. We are also going to check that the longitudinal centre of buoyancy (LCB) is more or less where we want it. But more of the latter later. If you used the block coefficient scheme things should be reasonable, but we must make sure.

What we have done in that displacement calculation is to work out the volume of water that is displaced by the hull when it is sitting down to LWL. The weight of that volume must equal the weight of the boat, and dividing by 35 converted cubic feet to tons (there are 35 cu. ft of sea water to the ton). If instead of dividing by 35 we had multiplied by 64 the answer would have been in pounds, assuming the boat was floating in sea water (a cubic foot of sea water weighs 64 lb). Thus the calculation would have been:

$$\text{Displacement} = \tfrac{2}{3} \times \text{CI} \times \text{Product total} \times 64 = \tfrac{2}{3} \times 2.83 \times 22.06 \times 64 = 2680 \text{ lb}$$

If the metric system had been used—and let's assume that the figures in the areas column were cubic metres and not cubic feet and that the distance between the stations was 2.83 metres—the displacement sum would be very similar, thus:

$$\text{Displacement} = \tfrac{2}{3} \times \text{CI} \times \text{Product total} = \tfrac{2}{3} \times 2.83 \times 22.06 = 41.7 \text{ cu. m}$$

That is 41 700 kilogrammes.

Note that CI is common interval or the distance apart of the stations, or sections. That figure is, of course, in either feet or metres.

Longitudinal Centre of Buoyancy

In the sum for LCB or longitudinal centre of buoyancy, the centre of area of the space occupied by the boat in the water was found. In effect the boat balances on that spot and if the fore and aft position of its centre of gravity were not directly over the centre of buoyancy the craft would tip forwards or backwards to make a differently-shaped hole in the water whose centre of area did line up with the centre of gravity. The sum for finding the LCB is precisely the same with the metric system. Assuming that the product figures were in square metres and the common interval was in metres also the LCB would lie 0.028 metres ahead of station 4.

The bottom cuts the waterline at stations 0 and 8, therefore there is no area at either station. This is generally the case with sailing boats but craft having immersed transoms will have an immersed area right back to the transom and so figures must be put in the appropriate columns. This ought to become clearer when other examples are studied.

Longitudinal Centre of Gravity

Finally, back to that LCB and LCG (longitudinal centre of gravity) thing. In theory, and it has been done in table 6, the fore and aft position of the centre of gravity ought to be worked out; but search your conscience and study the situation. We are dealing with the flattie shown in fig 4 at the moment. The LCG of the hull alone is nearly always just about on 'midships (station 4 here). We have cabins fore and aft of that position and a cockpit placed just about centrally so that the crew will normally be concentrated round 'midships. There are no undue weights at either end since this craft does not have an inboard nor a heavy anchor and chain. Water and fuel will probably be carried

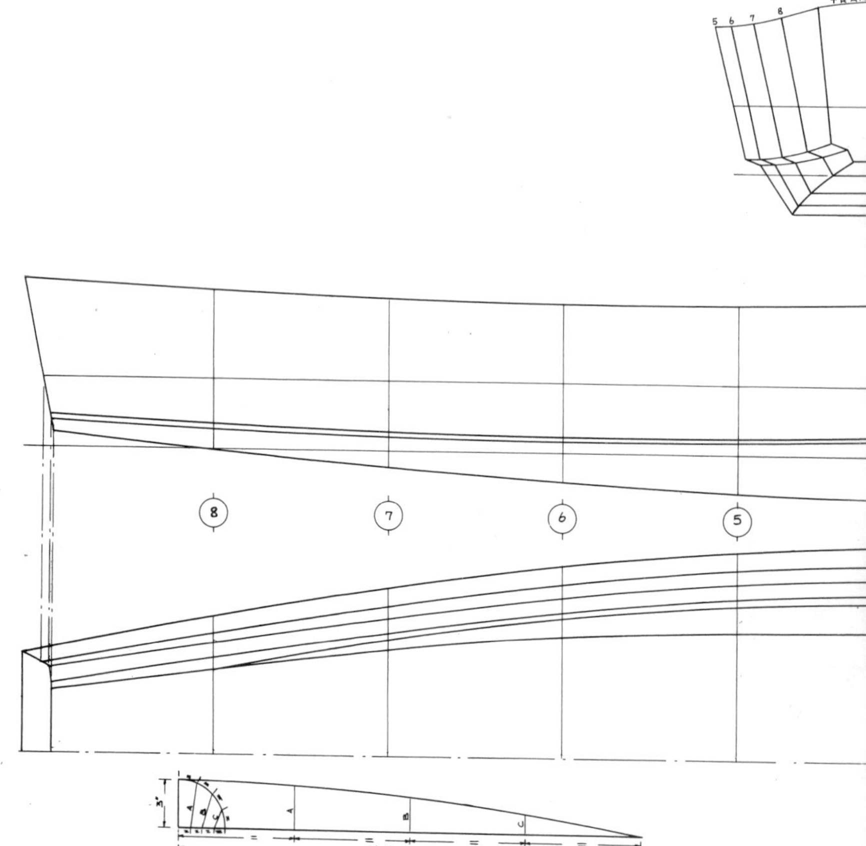

in portable tanks in the cockpit. All in all I think we can say that our position of the LCB will match up with LCG for all practical purposes especially considering that the crew weight is such a large proportion of the total, and crews tend to shift around. However, you can work it out if you have doubts and that table 6 demonstrates the method.

Position of LCB becomes important when dealing with high performance sailing craft and motor boats, but this will be covered when we come to examples of such boats. For general knockabout purposes the LCB should lie at 'midships of perhaps just a little aft of that point. The calculation showed that LCB here was fractionally forward of station 4, but so little that to all intents and purposes it was at 'midships, which is good enough. Bear in mind, though, that an LCB near 'midships implies a weight distribution whose centre is also near 'midships and that must be catered for in the layout.

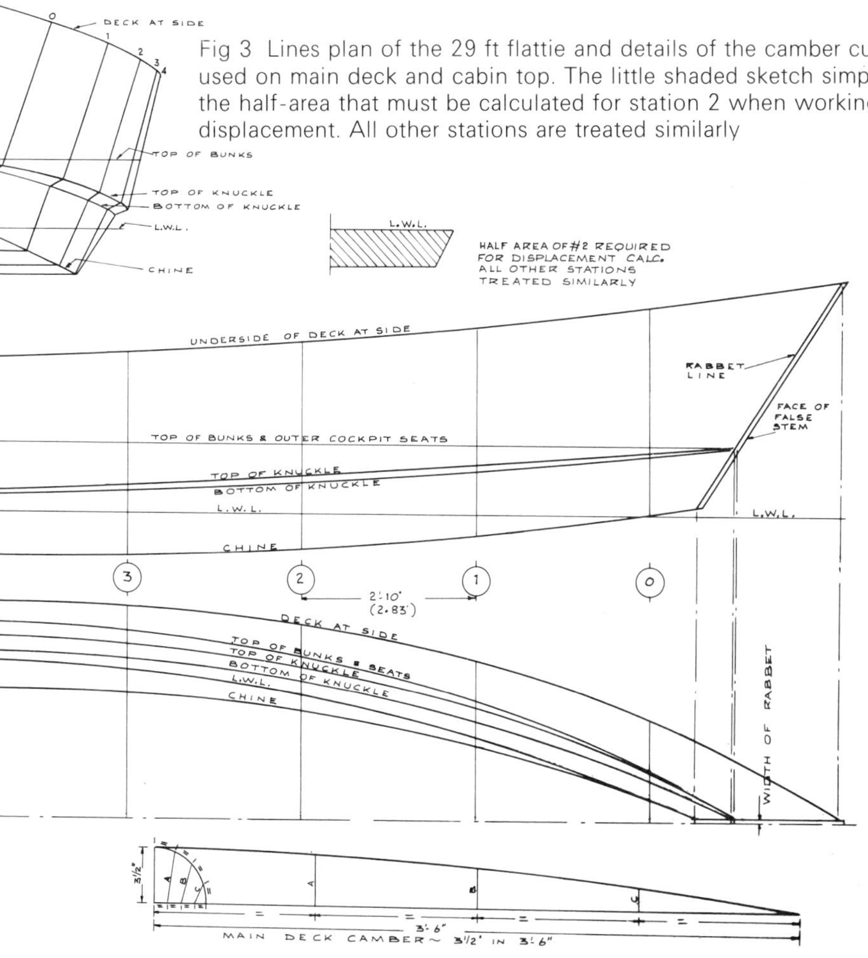

Fig 3 Lines plan of the 29 ft flattie and details of the camber curves used on main deck and cabin top. The little shaded sketch simply shows the half-area that must be calculated for station 2 when working out the displacement. All other stations are treated similarly

29 ft FLATTIE KETCH

Figs 3, 4, 5 and 6 apply. This one was designed for a South African gentleman (I use that word advisedly since he voluntarily paid me more than the agreed design fee!) for use on Vaal Dam. This is a large sheet

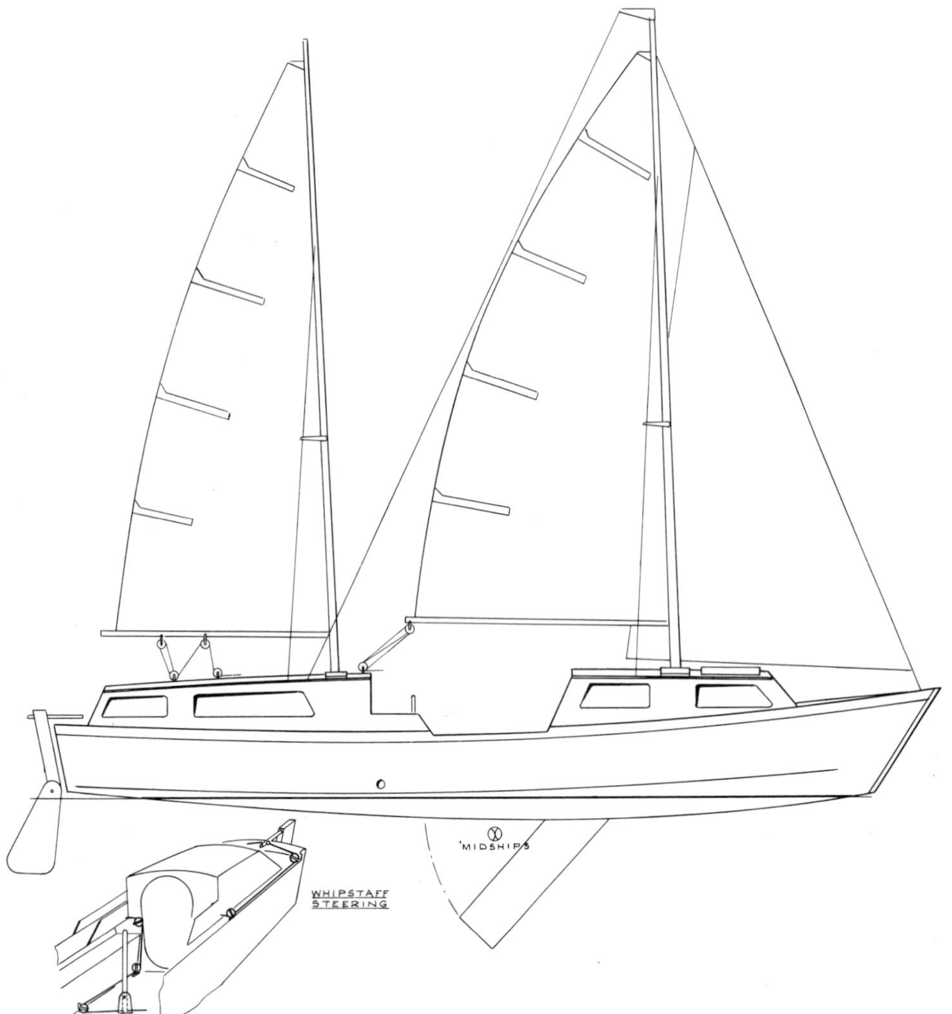

Fig 4 Outboard profile of the flattie and a sketch of the whipstaff steering. LOA 29 ft (8.8 m); LWL 22 ft 8 in. (6.9 m); beam 6 ft 8½ in. (2.05 m); beam WL 4 ft 10 in. (1.47 m); beam at bottom 4 ft (1.22 m); draught 8¼ in. (0.21 m); LCB 0.028 ft (0.008 m) fwd. of 'midships; disp. 1.2 tons (1220 kilos); C_B 0.57; Sail area 222 sq. ft (20.6 sq. m); sail area/displacement ratio 202

of water somewhere near Johannesburg and like all similar places can have a short, very steep sea running in a big wind. Clearly shoal draught is an advantage since shallow inlets and natural sheltered anchorages can be found at most states of water level in the dam. The craft was wanted for knockabout sailing, for use under outboard when the wind dropped and, in the owner's words as 'an Edwardian picnic barge'. The family intended to sleep aboard fairly frequently and it was to be built at home. Rather than go to the expense of getting special sails and spars the idea was to use standard dinghy gear as far as possible and to clear that point up straight away, the main is a Tempo mast and sail, while the mizzen comes from an Andy. The genoa is a 'one-off'.

As far as general hull form goes, it seemed to me advisable to keep the stem clear of the water, but only just. While a flattie may coast over big ocean waves comfortably enough, in a steep chop it is bound to slam particularly under power and the closer, and the less exposed bottom forward there is, the less rigorous should be the pounding. Immersing the stem altogether would be even better but that seems to detract from performance under sail. In any case, when sailing the boat is normally heeled and so presents an angle rather than a flat surface to the water forward.

Beam/Length Ratio. The ideal of between four and five beams to the length has already been mentioned but this does make for a craft rather too easily heeled for a young, inexperienced crew. So it seemed a good scheme to incorporate a sort of chine or knuckle the whole length of the boat just above the water line. Normally the vessel has the required beam/length ratio but as she heels the knuckle enters the water and

Fig 5 The structural scheme that could be employed for a flattie. The idea is to have a few major items that can be cut out to the correct size which when erected are self-aligning and can be used as a foundation on which to attach the rest of the structure

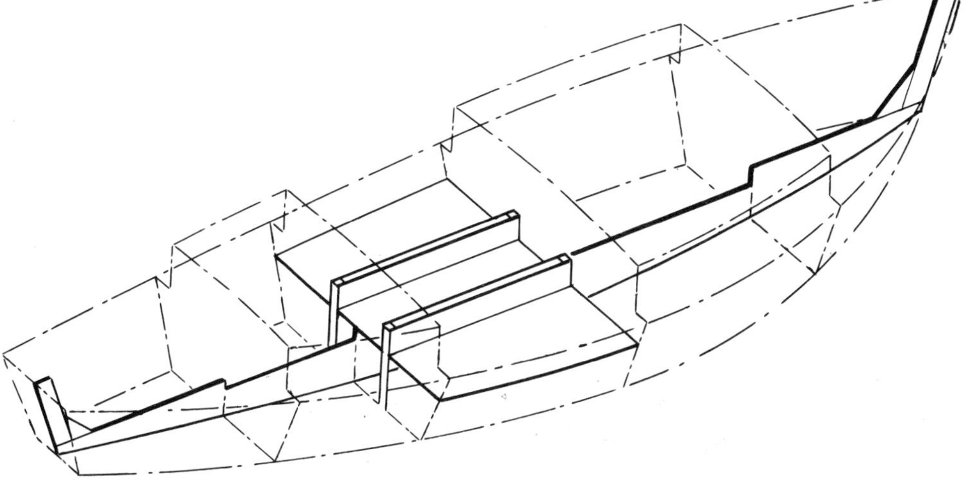

Fig 6 Some structural details for the sailing flattie

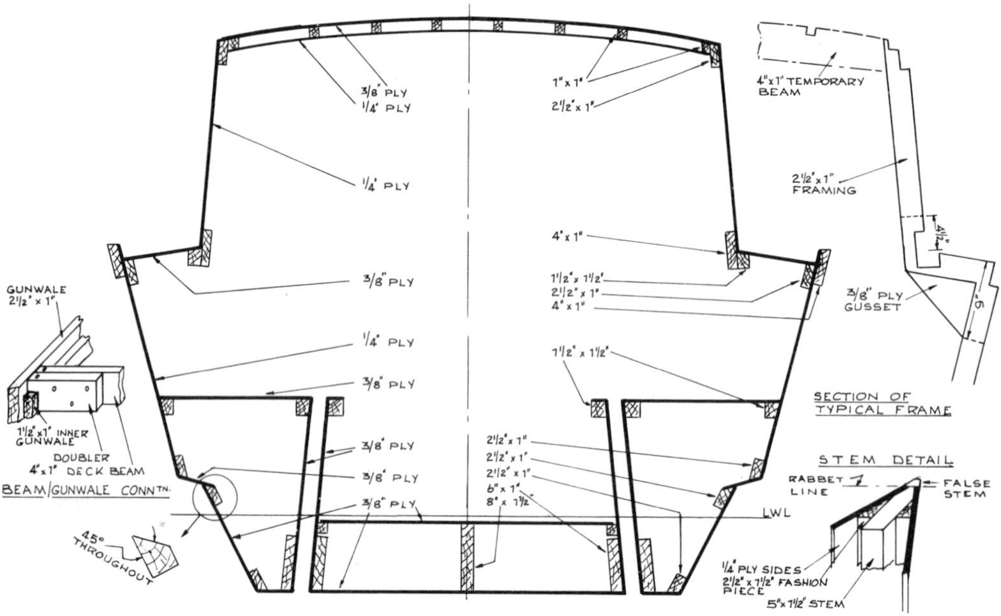

gives an added area of buoyancy. This should not affect sailing qualities unduly and would give greater peace of mind as the wind climbs up the scale. Naturally this knuckle complicates building somewhat but she is still easier to build than a normal single chine boat while a flat bottom does mean that you can get the accommodation sole very low while maintaining a worthwhile width.

Rudder and Centreboards. This flattie has whipstaff steering and a little sketch of the scheme is reproduced on fig 4. A tiller would have been impractical with an outboard rudder and wheel steering was considered a trifle ostentatious and expensive. The way it works can probably be deduced. By waggling the stick sideways the tiller follows suit and as long as the leads for the steering wires are strategically placed so that everything runs smoothly through big pulleys there is plenty of 'feel' in the system. It takes up little room in the cockpit which is good.

There are twin centreboards, as can be seen from the construction sketches, and these and the rudder are basically of thin mild steel plate (about 2 mm) sheathed in ply both sides. Large areas of lateral plane are needed on flatties to counteract their desire to travel sideways and though the total area of two centreboards would not be as effective as one board double the size, together they would probably be as good as something one and a half times their area in a single plate, while being a lot easier to arrange without cluttering up the accommodation.

With the coming of epoxy paints and putties the use of steel to reinforce timber structures such as rudders has become easy and practical. As long as the cut edge of the steel is properly ground smooth, the timber can be bolted through on a bed of epoxy putty. Similar paint

round the edges will seal things well and rust should be no problem.
Building System. It is purely personal fad as will become, I fear, increasingly obvious as you skim through this book, but I would go to great lengths to avoid the use of building moulds. Perhaps this fetish is carried too far, but for me at any rate the search for a level, flat piece of ground on which to laboriously erect, square and true building frames that are probably thrown away in the end, is the least inspiring of tasks. It seems much preferable to bash out various components in a shed or garage somewhere and then one fine spring day take the bits outside and assemble them into the structure of a boat in a matter of an hour or so. A flattie lends itself to this type of action, as does a catamaran, but more of that later. If nothing else, this instant assembly method of building raises gasps of admiration from the neighbours.

Fig 5 is a rough sketch showing the general approach used with a flat-bottomed vessel. Obviously, if the lines plan was drawn to a big enough scale, the centre line assembly of keel, stem and transom can be made direct from drawings. In a like manner so can the centreboard cases port and starboard—supposing there were two of these things.

Bulkheads can be cut out to the correct shape apart from bevelling and so, for instance, can the cockpit sole. On many craft bunk and locker fronts can be in one line and these, too, can be prefabricated. So, these are the sorts of things one hacks away at in the secret confines of your shed. Long structures such as the keel can have butt straps made and screw holes drilled but left for final assembly outside.
Erection. The first task when you stagger outside is to put the keel together, if necessary. Sight along it where it lies on the ground to make sure the various component curves are fair. Then drop the bulkheads over it and secure. These should be designed to be fastened on a sort of egg-box principle, slotted to take the keel. Next, if there are two centre-board cases, put them in. If they have been cut to the correct length they should square up the appropriate bulkheads but check as you go. In many instances they will not end on bulkheads at all but are slotted through them and can be continued as those bunk fronts, which can also be fastened home at this stage. A cockpit sole put in now will prevent twisting. When screwed and glued all these items produce a nice, rigid structure to which the chines and gunwales can be fastened and the whole can be rolled about for the fitting of sides and bottom.
Cabin Top. There were three pages of instruction concerning the order in which to install things on that 29-footer but the general scheme was that just outlined.

There is not much of particular interest in the construction details of the flattie, except that the method of building the cabin top perhaps deserves a mention. On a boat like this with very restricted headroom at the best of times, beams supporting a cabin top are a blasted nuisance. A sketch on fig 6 shows that the frames had temporary beams integral with them, so that with the bulkheads a proper shape for the cabin top was given. One inch by one inch battens were laid in notches and the top $\frac{3}{8}$ in. ply was glued and fastened to them. The temporary beams were then hacked away and the inner layer of $\frac{1}{4}$ in. ply fastened to the battens. Fig 6 shows the resulting structure which is strong, rigid, and above all, thin!

Deck Camber

Before leaving this ketch, have another glance at fig 3 for it shows how to draw deck camber. Select the amount of camber you think would be right for your application—such as 1 in. per foot of half beam. That means that if your craft had 6 ft beam the deck in the middle would be 3 in. higher than at the edge. Now draw a base line equal in length to the maximum half-beam and divide it into four equal parts. At one end draw a quarter-circle with radius equal to the camber selected and divide its base also into four equal parts. Next divide the arc of the quarter circle into yet another four equal parts and join lines as indicated. Transfer length A from the quarter circle to the appropriate upright on the half beam base line; do the same with length B and so on; and join the spots given. Normally the camber curve is drawn to a bigger scale than the rest of the lines plan for the sake of accuracy. For the amount of camber at any place narrower than maximum half-beam simply measure out the required distance and then down to the curve.

24 ft CANAL CRUISER

Another flattie, but this one a very different kettle of fish. Back in the dark ages of the mid-1960s when timber construction was still respectable, though only just, a company with a base on the canals asked me to design them a four-berth cruiser. This is the result. Only one was built because the firm eventually decided that rather than specialise in canal boats they would go in for multi-purpose craft in glass fibre and acquired a set of moulds for that purpose. However, this affair went pretty well and did all I had hoped, but as you can see the hull form would not be much use for high-speed travel offshore or, in fact, for any purpose other than a leisurely gambol over sheltered waters. In that role it is quite efficient for the transom ends clear of the water thereby avoiding the excessive low-speed resistance caused by an immersed transom and the great, curling wake that such a feature ensures. People are in business to make money, not boats, as a general rule and if they produce a craft which can be advertised as being suitable for low speeds on canals and rivers and high speeds in coastal waters then they can hope to attract quite a wide range of customers. The fact that the boat is not efficient in any of its possible settings will not bother the very great majority of owners.

Philosophising over, let me add one more aside before getting down to details. When this boat was launched a bloke from a yachting journal came up for the trials. Unfortunately he headed his account of these 'A Unique Canal Cruiser' or words to that effect and was talking about the hollow keel. The result of his well-intentioned efforts to get people to read the piece was my receiving a shoal of vaguely abusive letters telling me that the keel was not by any means unique and that so-and-so had used it in such-and-such a year. Well, ten thousand curses; I hadn't claimed any originality for that feature and the only satisfaction that could be had from the episode was that none of my lecturing correspondents had gone nearly far enough back over the years in their examples—so their heroes had feet of clay, too!

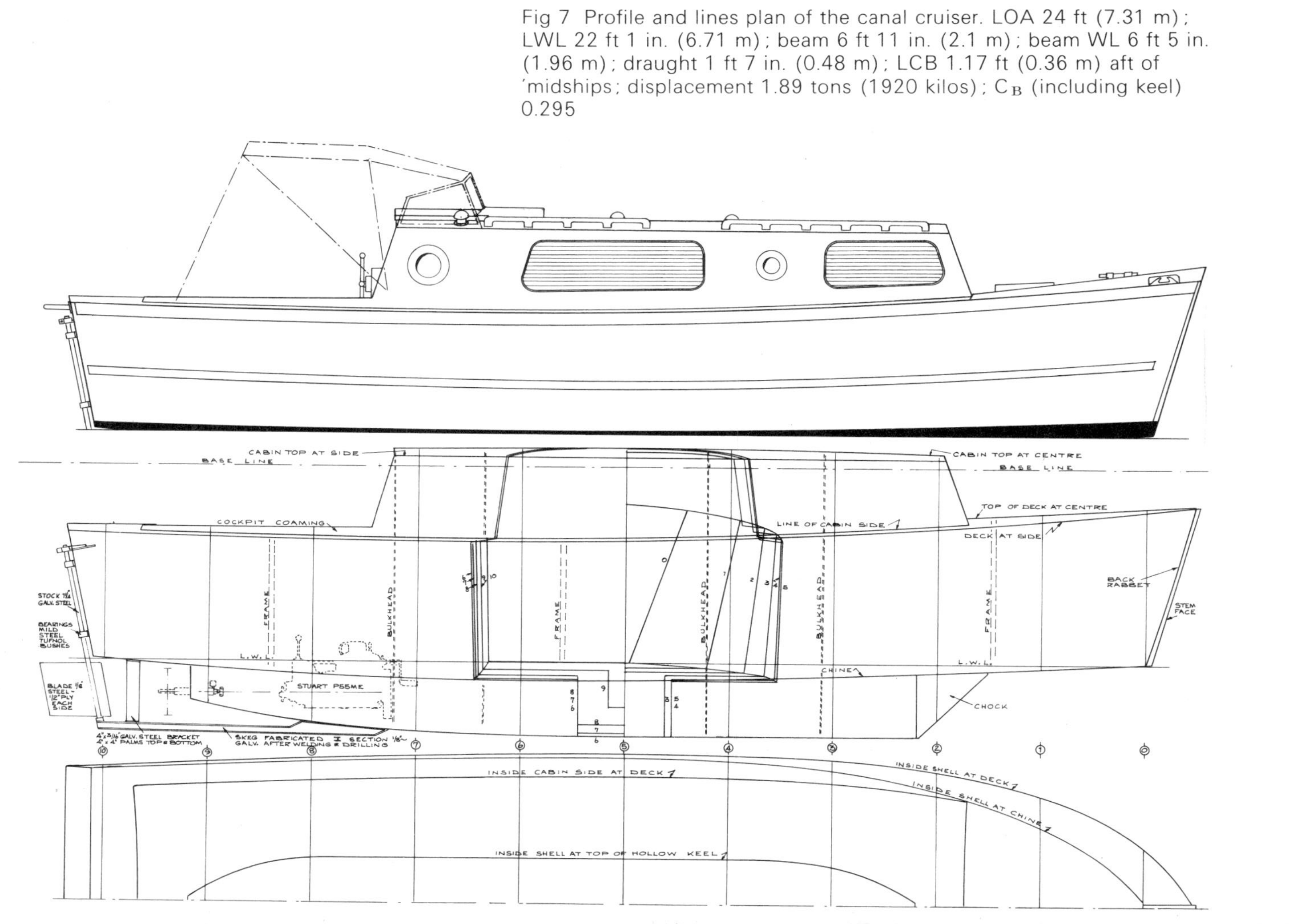

Fig 7 Profile and lines plan of the canal cruiser. LOA 24 ft (7.31 m); LWL 22 ft 1 in. (6.71 m); beam 6 ft 11 in. (2.1 m); beam WL 6 ft 5 in. (1.96 m); draught 1 ft 7 in. (0.48 m); LCB 1.17 ft (0.36 m) aft of 'midships; displacement 1.89 tons (1920 kilos); C_B (including keel) 0.295

I remember Charles Greene, now of Cruiser Kits, writing an article in *Yachting Monthly* shortly after the Second World War describing a sailing boat with a hollow keel he proposed building. I don't suppose even he was the first and in fact it is virtually impossible to come up with any entirely original ideas in yacht designing.

Anyway, the keel seemed a good idea on a canal cruiser which, strangely enough, sets quite a few problems for a designer. In the days when canals were used commercially to good advantage they were reasonably deep and the passage of fair numbers of heavily-laden carriers kept the channels clear. Now, though, anything much more than 2 ft draught is a definite drawback. There are various low bridges on the system and so one can't simply build upwards. In any case, one of the bad features of the modern, lightly-built vessel is that with very little in the water it tends to be blown about by the wind and can be a pig to handle, especially when going very slowly as it approaches a lock, for instance.

If a conventionally vee'd hull is used the sole line must be fairly high in the hull in order to achieve a decent width in what is already an accommodation very restricted by the 6 ft 11 in. maximum beam dictated by many lock sizes. And if the sole is high, so is the cabin top and we are back to the problems of bridges and windage.

Thus it seemed to me that if the populace thronging the craft could walk along the bottom of a hollow keel we would have the best possible solution. Fig 7 shows the result. On a boat of this type the main hull must be only lightly immersed with the keel providing most of the buoyancy.

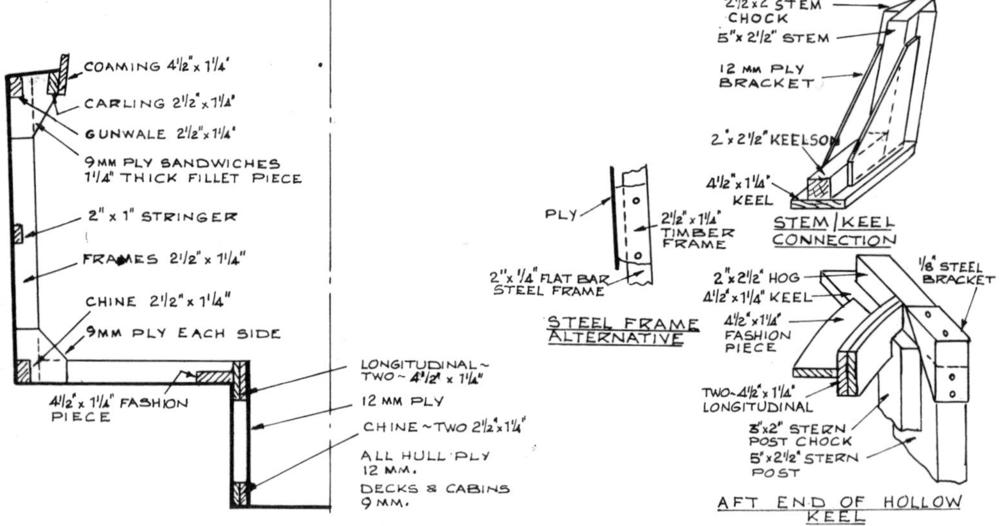

Fig 8 Canal cruiser structural details. Though this seemed strong enough for canal work I would prefer some steel framing on a vessel designed for the rough and tumble of life at sea. One suggested method is shown but another is sketched on fig 9

A weight calculation gave a figure of 1.80 tons and displacement from the lines plan is 1.89 tons so we were pretty close but on the right side in that, if anything, the craft would float slightly light. As a matter of interest the 8 hp Stuart Turner produced a cruising speed of around 5 knots and a maximum of 6½ knots, both of which figures are suitable for canal work.

Structure. There is one snag with this shape if it is intended that the cabin sole shall be along the bottom of the keel and that is that it is very difficult to build the boat strongly enough in wood. Fig 8 shows the method used and it seemed satisfactory for canal work but if a seagoing craft were the intention I think the strains on the hollow keel when under way would soon cause leaks to develop round the keel/hull connection, if nothing worse. There seem to be two possible ways out of the difficulty. One is to use a few steel frames in the manner sketched on fig 8. The frames would be of flat bar but would be set sufficiently inboard of the hull sides and bottom for timber stringers to pass outside them. These stringers would be fastened to the timber

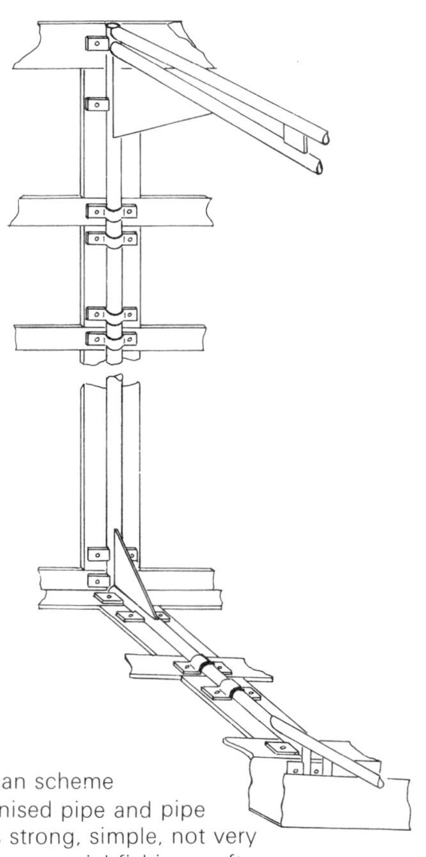

Fig 9 This is an American scheme utilising standard galvanised pipe and pipe clamps for framing. It is strong, simple, not very beautiful and used on commercial fishing craft

frames which are, in turn, bolted to the steel bars. The steelwork need not then be terribly accurate though with welded and possibly bracketed corners it should give all the strength needed.

Tubular Framing. The second method might be to work on the system shown in fig 9 which an American firm, Marine View Boat Building Co., Tacoma, Washington use on commercial fishing boats. Galvanised piping forms the framework and pipe clamps support stringers, chines, gunwales and so forth. The clamps ensure that these longitudinal items are more or less self-aligning. In the sketch reproduced pipes cross the hollow keel which would make walking along it something of a problem. However, it would probably be feasible to put in a further horizontal pipe a few inches above the one that forms the bottom framing and then weld a vertical down from it, past the bottom frame and along the hollow keel side. Something like the method shown for the side decks, in fact. The Marine View craft are planked in two or three skins of exterior, not marine, ply and subsequently sheathed in epoxy/glass.

Incidentally the canal cruiser was built upside down in the conventional manner and that is why a base line is shown some way above the deck. This is really the floor line and dimensions from that line were given to appropriate bits of the framework. There is more on base lines when we look at a rigid-bottom inflatable in the next chapter. Just having a quick glance at the plans that illustrate the boats, it occurs to me that I ought to mention that the strut behind the propeller is off-centre just enough to allow the prop shaft to be removed. Other than that I can't think of anything else very interesting to say about it.

Hatches

Both this craft and the 29 ft ketch discussed previously had lifting hatches and fig 10 illustrates the type. These have double coamings and were developed by Maurice Griffiths. Whereas most lifting and virtually all sliding hatches leak, this model is a considerable improvement since water finding its way over one coaming simply falls into a waterway and drains out. The overall height of a hatch like this should be about 4 in., though the higher the better in practice.

Decks and Associated Structures

Both the boats so far shown had simple ply decks, sheathed as required. Traditionally, though, decks were of individual planks of wood spiked to the beams and sometimes, in high-class construction, to each other as well. With this form of building they added a little to the longitudinal strength of the vessel but their main function was to provide something to walk on and, hopefully, to keep the rain out. They could play no part in holding the two sides of the boat together nor in preventing those two sides twisting in relation to each other. The deck beams had to do all that work and so were braced to the hull with lodging knees (whose arms were horizontal) and hanging knees with vertical arms.

When reliable marine ply came on the market the situation was transformed. With stout butt straps glued and screwed in position the deck took over much of the burden from the beams which now became simple supports for the ply. But ply decking on its own is not very attractive for the outer veneer is quite thin and is quickly worn down to the glue line by the constant pounding of feet so that some sort of

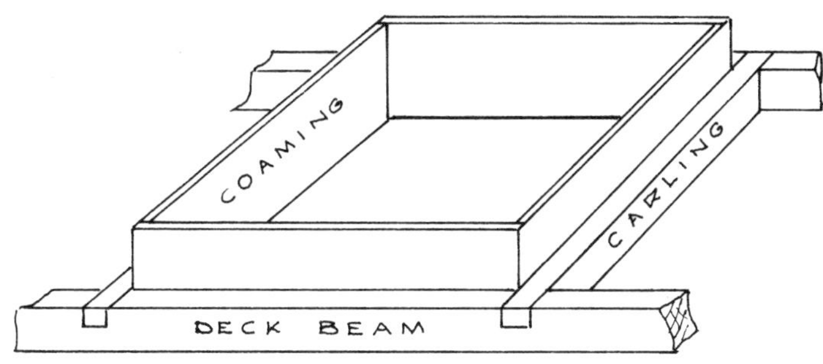

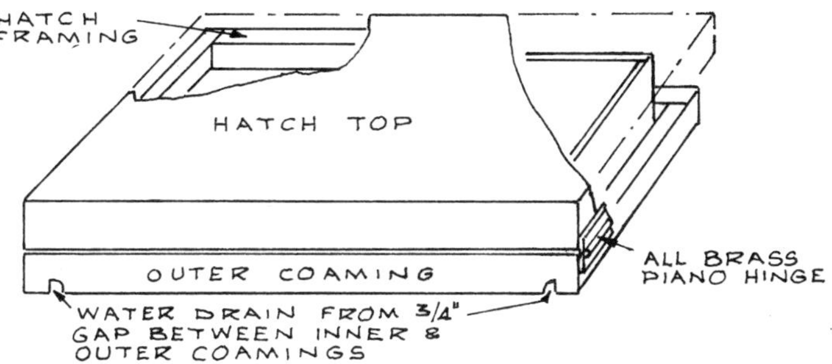

Fig 10 The Maurice Griffiths-developed lifting hatches. Water driving under the hatch top falls into the gap between the two coamings and drains away

sheathing has to be used. In its simplest form this consists of painted canvas and this is an effective, cheap and simple solution. We have had it on one of our boats for a couple of years now and it shows few signs of wear. It comprises an old sheet put down on wet Liquid Lino and subsequently painted with a couple more coats of the same stuff. Marine glue is an alternative to paint as a base but lately such cheap answers have been supplanted by nylon or glass fibre sheathing in conjunction with resorcinal glues or epoxy or polyester resins. Of the latter, epoxy resins stick better to wood than the polyesters. In top-class construction plank decks are still used, generally laid over a ply base for strength purposes. Such a deck looks excellent and provides natural non-skid properties. The top sheathing is normally glued to the ply with resorcinal, though it may be laid on a synthetic rubber base. The main trouble with such decks is any leaks that develop are fiends incarnate when it comes to tracing their source, while contemplating a layer of water between the two skins in such cases is not conducive to happy, dreamless nights.

Cutting Timber for Decks. Fig 11 shows various types of deck structure, but to kick off with let us cast our eyes towards the top left-hand corner where are sketches of two ways of converting timber from the round. Actually there are three ways, the third being termed plain-sawn, where simple parallel planks are cut from the log. Rift sawing is best for softwoods like pine, and quarter-sawn is what Lloyds recommend for all decking. Timber cut this way wears better and shrinks more evenly. It is worth specifying it if you can, should you be designing a good-class yacht, though it will cost more. More than likely plain sawn is all that can be purchased easily and in that case the annular rings should be laid concave side downwards. If intending to sheath a ply deck with timber it is worth going to the expense of getting a really superior timber like teak. With that your fears of leaks and rot should be much reduced. Frankly I wouldn't use anything else. If it is too expensive sheathe the other way with anything from canvas to nylon.

Hanging Knees. The sketches over the letter A demonstrate fairly basic but perfectly sound constructional methods. This sort of thing was used on the 29 ft ketch. Also shown is a hanging knee which effectively ties the deck and associated structure down to the hull. Hanging knees are used mainly on sailing craft these days where the strains are greater than on power boats and are found principally on beams in the way of

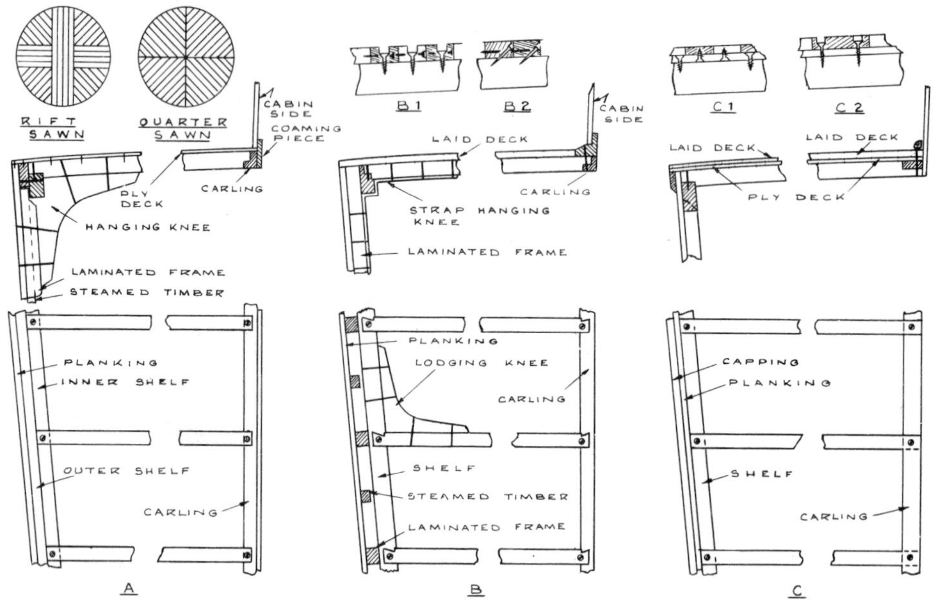

Fig 11 Some hull side/deck/cabin side connections in timber plus details of timber deck and ply deck fastenings to beams

masts. Fig 59 near the end of the book is of a modern, timber-built yacht and in that example there are hanging knees on each of the three beams around the main and mizzen masts. These knees may be of timber, usually laminated, or of metal straps. The deck on the sketches over A is meant to be plain ply.

Next along, over B, comes a laid deck. That is a deck consisting of planking only. For strength purposes it doesn't matter whether the planks run fore and aft or follow the sweep of the deck line. The planks should be nailed to each other and either spiked or screwed to the beams. The deck/cabin side connection is a rather superior and more expensive construction than that shown over A. Its main advantage is that if ply cabin sides are used the bottom edge of the ply is kept out of the puddles. If it is not, water tends to creep up the end grain and stains the timber. This means that a varnished side will speedily have to be painted since it is impossible to remove the stain marks. Also shown on fig 11 B are lodging knees and dovetailed beams both of which features are associated with plain, laid decks. The use of lodging knees has been mentioned.

Dovetails. Cut in a beam a dovetail goes some way to ensuring that the beam does not pull away from the gunwale; they are always cut on the side nearest 'midships and are not nearly so common today where ply fastened to both beams and deck edge structure does the same job only better. The sketches over C show some more variations and this time we have a laid/ply deck. C1 considers the case where the ply is less than half the total deck thickness. Here the ply must be separately fastened to each plank with the whole lot finally fastened down from above. If the ply is over half the total thickness of the deck (C2) it need not be separately fastened to the planking over it. The lower sketches show more beam/hull/cabin side themes. The idea of taking the decking over the hull planking and fastening it down to a capping outside the shell is most often found on cold-moulded, ply or double-diagonal planked craft where the top edge of the planking would hardly be suitable for screw fastenings. If this system is used a hefty outside rubbing strake must be incorporated on the hull lower down. You can imagine the consequences otherwise. A gently rocking boat whose gunwale is at the same height as another boat's or the edge of a jetty and gaping holes could soon be lifted at the perimeter of the deck. The cabin side/deck connection of fig 11 C is a simple one that relies heavily on a quarter-round beading maintaining a watertight joint. If it doesn't, leaks are the inevitable result though if the decks were glassed or sheathed in some other way and the sheathing taken up under that beading you could feel a bit more optimistic about staying dry below.

The variations shown may seem a bit indigestible and the explanations a trifle compressed. All of them work, though, and really you can choose which you like and whichever suits your requirements best. People have prejudices, of course, and mine are always to take the simplest way out, but for each shining advantage claimed by an adherent for one particular method an equally well-informed opponent to the scheme could be found. You can combine features of one sketch with features from another.

Caulking a Laid Deck. And finally on this theme of decks. Fig 12 shows a couple more details concerning planked decks laid on ply. The two caulking methods are for synthetic filling compounds but manufacturers of the stuff will normally make their own recommendations if approached and these could vary from maker to maker. It will be seen that it is not very good to lay a deck less than $\frac{5}{8}$ in. (15 mm) thick if only because there must be a decent bit of screw left in the deck itself and the dowel over it needs to be reasonably long if it is not to have a tendency to pop out.

Anyway, we can now leave niggling constructional details for a space as we're off on an examination of the slightly more sophisticated single chine hull form.

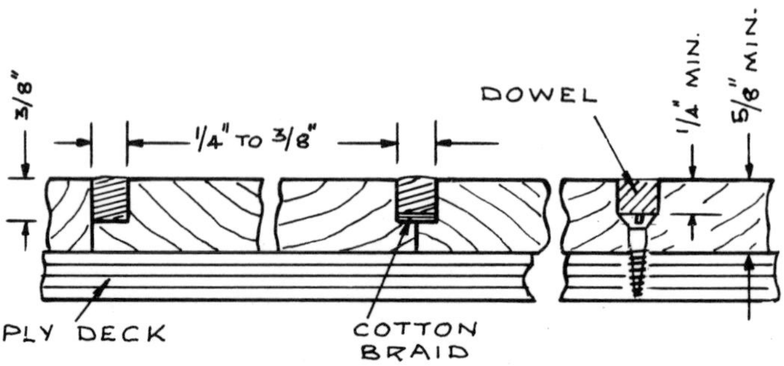

Fig 12 Two methods of preparing a deck for synthetic caulking compounds

2. Single Chine Forms

The advantages a hard chine, or vee-bottomed craft, has over a flattie are that there is a triangular section sticking into the water and this means that the vessel can have more draught for any given area of underwater body; the boat is less liable to sideslip across the water; and is less liable to pound in a head sea. A chine form can have more beam without disastrous consequences and, indeed, it is a very respectable shape. Any craft destined to run at planing speeds for most of the time must have this form—though more on that subject later—while even for comparatively slow-speed yachts it is only slightly less efficient than a round bilge. When marine ply came on the market as a reliable boat-building material we saw a great many hard chine vessels designed to take advantage of the ease of building afforded by the ply. If we now see fewer, the reason is mainly that it is not a very suitable form for glassfibre construction. This needs lots of curves to strengthen what is inherently rather an un-stiff material. Anyway, thoughts on G.R.P. come later.

Planimeters. The same tools of the trade are needed for chine craft as for flatties and working out underwater areas for the displacement calculation can be done by dividing the submerged parts of the sections into triangles and rectangles. This is a rather tedious task, however, and if funds run to it a planimeter, which measures areas, will speed operations considerably. Two types are available. The first has a fixed scale and usually measures at 1 in. = 1 ft, or 1 : 1000 in the metric system. If your plan had been drawn to a different scale, multiply the answer by the square of the inverted scale. That sounds grand but does not convey much information, so two examples. . . .

You had a lines plan drawn at $1\frac{1}{2}$ in. = 1 ft, let us say. That is $\frac{3}{2}$ in. = 1 ft. To get the correct answer from a fixed scale planimeter, multiply the area products total in the displacement calculation by $\frac{2^2}{3^2}$ which is $\frac{4}{9}$. If the scale had been $\frac{3}{4}$ in. = 1 ft the multiplier would have been $\frac{4^2}{3^2}$ which is $\frac{16}{9}$. On the metric system, if a lines plan had been drawn to a scale of 1 : 15, multiply the area products total by $15^2 = 225$; if 1 : 10 by $10^2 = 100$ and so on. Table 4 gives examples of displacement calculations on both systems of measurement where this has had to be done. The second, more expensive type of planimeter, can be adjusted to measure to the scale you have used.

The first example in this chapter is a 15 ft 8 in. single chine sailing dinghy about which there is not going to be very much to say. On the other hand there is room for some comments on sailing performance in general so here goes.

Performance Under Sail

Most people who read this will have heard in a general way of the limiting speed on a sailing boat being governed by the craft's length. This limit does not apply to some performance dinghies, about which more will be said in this section, but otherwise is tied up with something called Speed/Length Ratio. This is the speed of the vessel in knots divided by the square root of its waterline length in feet, or $V/\sqrt{L}$.

Limiting Speed. Without going into reasons it can be taken that the length of the main wave generated by the boat's passage through the water is controlled solely by the speed of the craft and that at a speed/length ratio of 1:34 there will be a crest of that wave at the bow and another at the stern. We could now put a figure or two in the formula and get an answer in knots. Let us assume a yacht 25 ft on the waterline. The sum would then be:

$$1.34 = \frac{V}{\sqrt{25}} \text{ or } V = 1.34 \times \sqrt{25} = 1.34 \times 5 = 6.7 \text{ knots}$$

Thus at 6.7 knots there would be a crest at the bow and another at the transom of this length yacht. If speed were increased that aft crest would move away astern since wave length would increase and the stern of the vessel would dip down into a gradually deepening trough. Its attitude would be bows-up, stern-down and it would be virtually sailing uphill. To overcome this unhappy state of affairs power must be considerably increased to allow it to climb the hill and sit on that bow crest. All this is a rather simplified explanation of the proceedings but is fairly readily understandable, I hope. A vessel powered by sails is generally unable to achieve the necessary thrust for this uphill work and its speed is thus limited to a speed/length ratio of 1.34. In fact, it might exceed this by a small amount because at a ratio of, say 1.4 the hill is still not a very steep one.

A heavy boat will make a bigger wave than a light one of the same length and thus it must also be steeper since the distance between the crests will be the same. It follows that a lightweight machine like a racing dinghy whose sails can generate quite a lot of power balanced by the weight of the crew sitting out to one side is more likely to succeed in this uphill struggle than any other type of sailing vessel.

If we want to design a really fast wind-powered machine we would make it long, thin and light and arrange for moveable ballast to be sited as far outside the gunwale as possible. Length ensures that the limiting speed/length ratio is still quite fast and thinness and lightness go together in producing a shallow wave, easily climbed.

A Bit of History. Though some of the figures are now disputed, presumably by those who are naturally disputatious, the old-time sailing ships achieved pretty high speeds though still well within the limiting speed/length ratio. *Champion of the Seas,* a 252 ft American-built clipper, is said to have made a day's run of 465 miles in 1854, for instance, while the slightly smaller *James Bain* (226 ft) once logged 21 knots. *Red Jacket* covered 3185 miles in 10 consecutive days and *Melbourne* averaged 300 miles per day for 17 consecutive days. Even when steam came on the scene in the form of ships which could normally guarantee an arrival date within small limits, which the clippers and their kind could not, they were still not necessarily faster in short bursts. Thus in 1888 *Cutty Sark* doing 17 knots overhauled the mail steamer *Britannia* when she was at her maximum of 16 knots approaching Melbourne. That must have been quite an occasion. *Thermopylae* twice did the 14,000 mile Australia–London run in 60 days. She was 212 ft in length—just about the same as *Cutty Sark*—but the fact that the voyage could equally well take over 100 days effectively spelled the end for these marvellous vessels. But enough of these historical asides . . .

The sailing boats in this chapter are both dinghy-sized and we will concentrate on performance factors that influence this type of craft. A bigger yacht is shown in Chapter 4, where design considerations for that type of vessel will be discussed. It seems to me better to do things that way than skip endlessly from page to page hunting for illustrations of a particular feature.

Anyway, dinghies; and apologies are due for the bits of maths that follow which involve raising numbers to odd powers. Recruit your bright young son if you have forgotten how to use the log.log.scale on a slide rule or reduce the intricacies of a log. table to actual recognisable numbers.

Sail Area and Displacement Ratios

There are two ratios or coefficients involved; one being the sail area/displacement ratio and the other the displacement/length ratio. These are:

$$\text{Sail area/displacement ratio} = \frac{SA}{D^{\frac{2}{3}}}$$

$$\text{Displacement/length ratio} = \frac{D}{(\frac{L}{100})^3}$$

That bit about $D^{\frac{2}{3}}$ means that you square the number and then find the cube root of the result. Where $(\frac{L}{100})^3$ is concerned, divide the length in feet by 100 and then cube the answer. D is displacement in tons, which to all intents and purposes can be said to equal 1 metric tonne or 1000 kilos. In our case it is 2240 lb.

Table 3 shows those ratios worked out for a number of different dinghies with the addition of the Class A scow, which is really a very overgrown dinghy using its crew members as ballast, and the ocean racer *Black Soo* to show what can be achieved with a stripped out racing machine. Clearly we need a high figure for the sail area/displacement ratio and a low one for the displacement/length ratio. *Black Soo* had ¾-ton outside ballast which messes up her ratios—and must do on every craft that does not rely purely on shifting human weight to keep it upright. The New Zealand Skiff normally carries a five-man crew which rather spoils her displacement/length ratio but this is more than compensated for by the staggering sail area they commonly set and which shoves that ratio way up in the air. If you were designing a performance sailing dinghy these, then, are the ratios to aim for. But do they tell the whole story? No, sir, they do not and for further astounding revelations read on. When I first deduced the scheme that follows I felt inspired to write about it in a yachting journal. The response was distinctly deflating for only one reader bothered to comment and he informed me that it was a load of old rubbish and that the coefficients could not be used in the way shown. He then proceeded to demonstrate how it should be done but I couldn't honestly see what had been achieved after all the sums had been done (correctly?). So I am unrepentant because for some weird reason the scheme seems to work and I only pass on the remarks as a possible warning. In fact this is a slightly simplified version of the original, though it is unaltered in concept.

Dinghy Performance. By using the sail area and displacement ratios already worked out an attempt is made to predict one dinghy's performance as compared to another. Naturally such fundamentals as a basically fast hull and an efficient rig have to be assumed for we are only concerned with the relationships between sail area, length and displacement. Displacement is always taken as that of the craft in sailing trim with the crew aboard, and length as overall length.

It is all horribly simple. First, divide the Sail Area/Displacement ratio by 10. Next take the Displacement/Length ratio away from 100 and add the two numbers.

Here is an example, using the 17 ft International Canoe. The Sail Area ratio was 360. Divide that by 10 and the answer is 36. The Displacement ratio was 32. Taken away from 100 that gives 68. Add the two and the answer is $68 + 36 = 104$.

If the same thing was done for the Flying Dutchman the number would be 103.3, which is virtually the same as the Canoe's. Though the Dutchman is nearly 3 ft longer than the Canoe we might expect, from the coefficient figures, that it should be just about as fast and this is confirmed by their having nearly identical Portsmouth Yardsticks. Fig 13 shows the sums worked out for all the dinghies mentioned, plus the 505, plotted against Portsmouth Yardsticks and as can be seen there is a reasonable measure of agreement. Incidentally, the figure for the National 12 is given as—19.7. Though odd, this is correct, for the Displacement/Length Ratio was 145. Take that from 100 and you get −45. Add the Sail Area/Displacement ratio and the answer is $25.3 - 45 = -19.7$.

So, one way to see whether a projected design was likely to be faster than some rival class would be to work the ratios and compare. On this theme, it is interesting to see how Uffa Fox's two-man sliding seat canoe of the 1930s measured up to the class he hoped to beat. He had already made a timed run of 16.3 knots on the Medina, at Cowes, in his International Canoe. To achieve a higher speed he built a 20-footer on the same lines, increased sail area from 107 to 120 sq. ft and equipped the craft with two sliding seats to add power in a good blow. He admits that he hoped for 20 knots but in the end found that

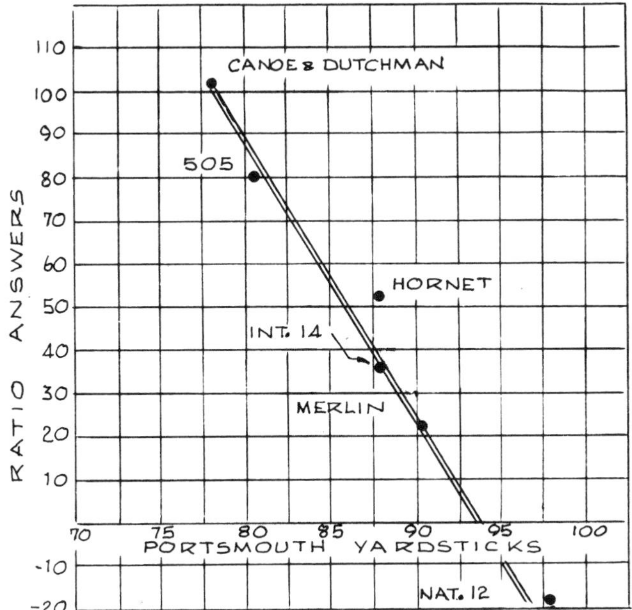

Fig 13 The answers found from working out sail area/displacement and displacement/length ratios for a selection of dinghies plotted against Portsmouth Yardsticks. As Portsmouth Yardsticks are modified from time to time those shown may not be precisely correct

the new boat was not quite as speedy as the International Canoe. If you work out the ratios and fiddle with them as indicated, the final figure is just about 100, which shows that the result in practice might have been predicted in theory. If, on the other hand, this 20-footer had been made a single-hander with the sail area left at 120 sq. ft and assuming that one man could handle that increase in area on a longer boat, which seems likely, the final answer would have been 110, indicating a faster vessel by a reasonable margin. The moral appears to be that weight is all-important and that a long, light single-hander is likely to be rather faster than a beamy, powerful dinghy requiring a heavy crew to cope with large areas of sail. The sail area of a Flying Dutchman is 190 sq. ft, yet she is no faster than a 17 ft Canoe and is probably slower than a single-hander of her own length setting only 120 sq. ft.

Fairing the Lines

Not everyone wants to design a flat-out racing machine so attention will now be turned to more mundane shapes. To start off with, fig 14 demonstrates the various measurements that must be made to correspond

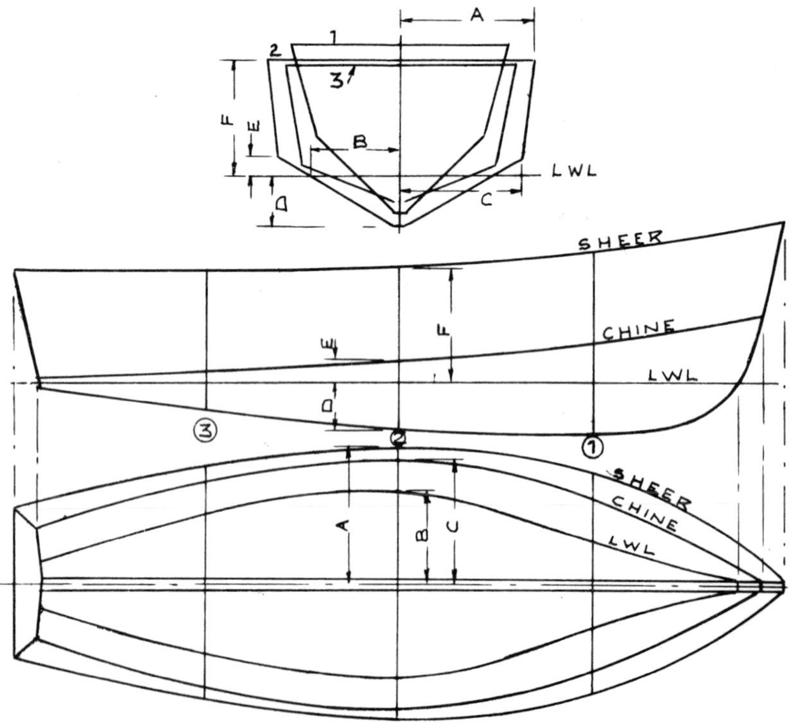

Fig 14 The dimensions lettered A to F must correspond on station 2 for a single chine craft. Naturally every other station is treated the same way

on a single chine hull. Again, both sides of the hull in plan and sectional views have been drawn for illustration and only station 2 is considered, though, of course, the same agreement must be achieved on every station. On this sketch the LWL (load waterline) has also been drawn in and its half-breadths in plan and section are indicated by the letter B. Here it has been assumed, for clarity, that the chine is above the LWL throughout. This might happen on a power boat but is unlikely on a single chine sailing craft as a glance at the plans of the boats in this chapter will show. Normally the LWL in plan will take up a fair curve forward until it hits the chine which is dipping down below the water. Aft of this it will again take up a fair curve but the two curves, forward and aft, are normally somewhat divergent. This looks odd on a drawing but is quite usual and if the divergence is not excessive is perfectly acceptable.

15 ft 8 in. SAILING DINGHY

We built this one a few years ago for family use. Its main aim was as a single-hander but on occasion it has carried considerably more crew than that. Since we tend to live in the wilds where a sailing dinghy of any kind is a rarity there have been no opportunities to test speed against any recognised classes but she appears to go pretty well.

As with a lot of our boats, length is governed by ply sizes and since two 8 ft sheets produce a dinghy a little under 16 ft long, that is what we have. The rig is perhaps unusual, being what I suppose could be called a fully-battened balanced lug. This was an experiment which has worked out satisfactorily. First of all it is easy to make a mast up to about 14–15 ft in length for suitable planks can be found at any timber merchant and screwed and glued together to form a box, a decidedly cheap spar emerges. Similarly if scrap ply is employed, as it was on this dinghy, and even allowing for shifting the butt joints out of line with one another, two 8 ft lengths can form one side of a 14 ft mast (or boom or gaff or whatever you like). Once you climb above that size there is either a difficult search for suitable timber or scarph joints have to be cut to join two lengths together and that is a nuisance.

Because the normal one-man crew was quite light and we used this boat on lakes where the wind is bound to be flukey, it was felt that setting the normal sliding gunter would raise the centre of effort of the sail rather too high for comfort. Clearly a low centre of effort will produce less tipping than a high one and on a lake sliding seats and trapezes are best avoided. With these contraptions you tend to find yourself several feet out from the gunwale when the wind suddenly decides to drop to nothing or veer through 90 degrees. The battens were meant to induce an odd-shaped sail to set well, which they do.

Originally the mast was stepped unstayed but after a season when it often bent through graceful, though alarming, arcs, one shroud per side plus a forestay were added for peace of mind. The bottom is $\frac{3}{8}$ in. (9 mm) ply and the topside $\frac{1}{4}$ in. (6 mm) ply. There are no frames but there are two stringers per side along the bottom. Hull weight is getting on for 300 lb which is considerable but the boat is normally hauled up a rocky shore when sailing is over and we felt that strength was advisable. This dinghy was built conventionally, with building moulds set on a flat floor. Fig 17 illustrates the monster. The strange upwards protrusion forward is a strong beam for the mast. The lines plan is shown on fig 15 and though these are basically normal sailing dinghy lines with the transom clear of the water and a flat run aft there are strange-looking lines driving through to the crossing points of chine and stations and they deserve an explanation.

Conical Projection

On all the chine boats illustrated in this book, whether single or double chine, the conical projection of the bottom is shown. You can, if you like, ignore that altogether and simply draw straight line sections; that is, straight lines join keel to chine. On craft built of, say, thinnish ply a bit of muscle power will generally force the material down to where you have intended it to go though there could then be quite a

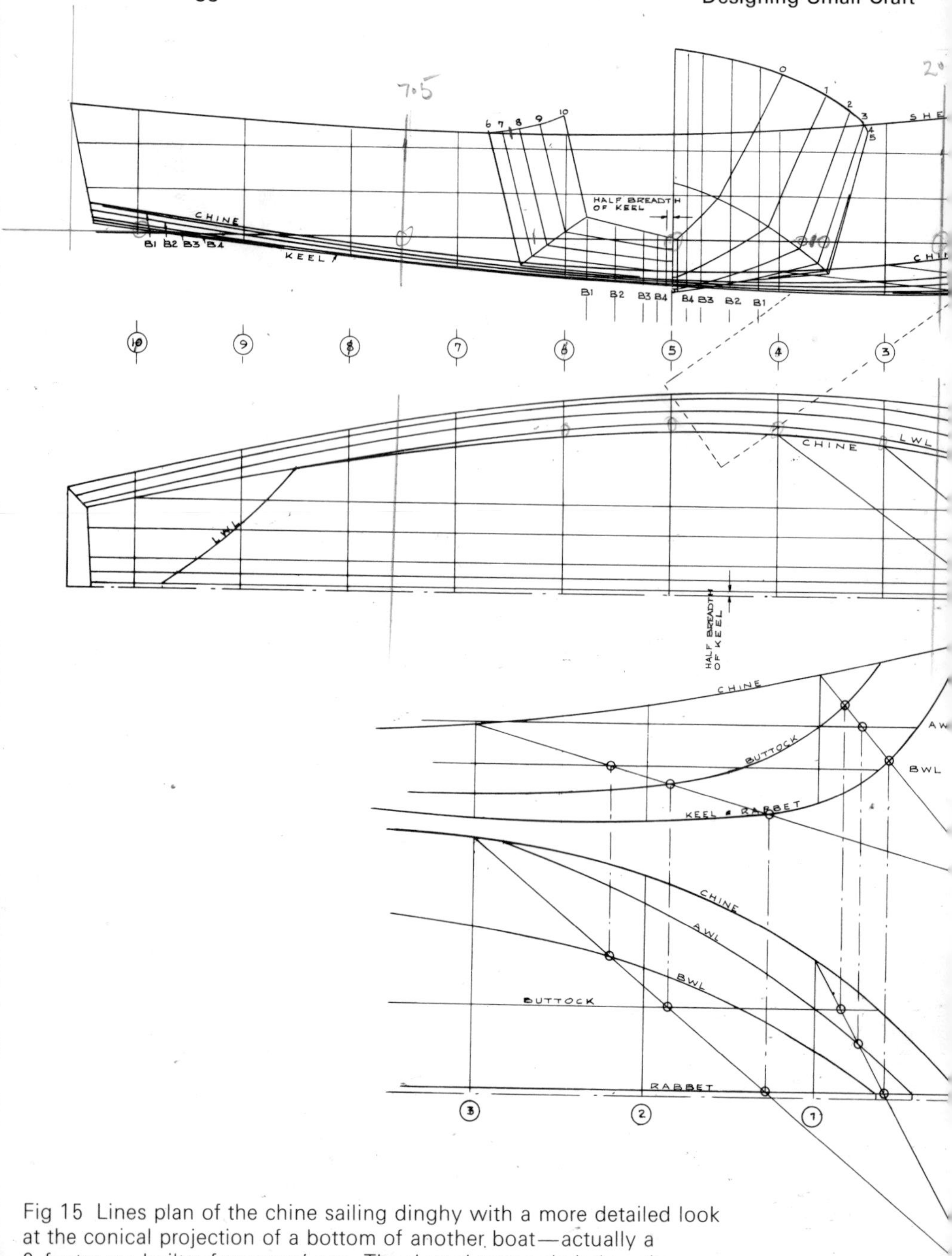

Fig 15 Lines plan of the chine sailing dinghy with a more detailed look at the conical projection of a bottom of another boat—actually a 9-footer we built a few years' ago. The dotted rectangle below the profile view of the lines plan is the centreboard

strain on the fastenings. However, if you cut a piece of cardboard to roughly the same shape as the bottom between keel and chine and twisted it to the appropriate curves you would see that the sections, particularly forward, are bent and not straight at all. What a conical projection does is to predict the curves on the sections while at the

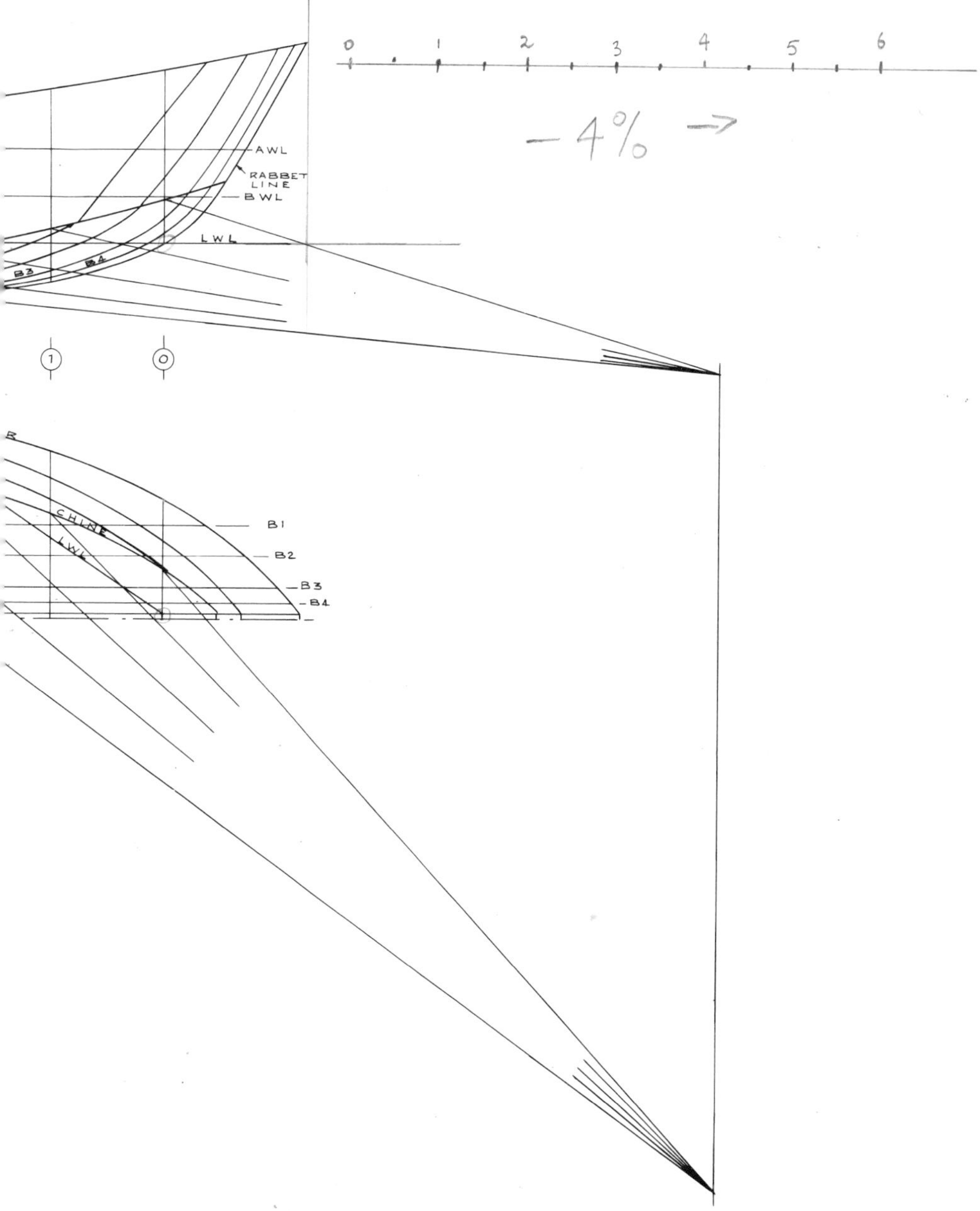

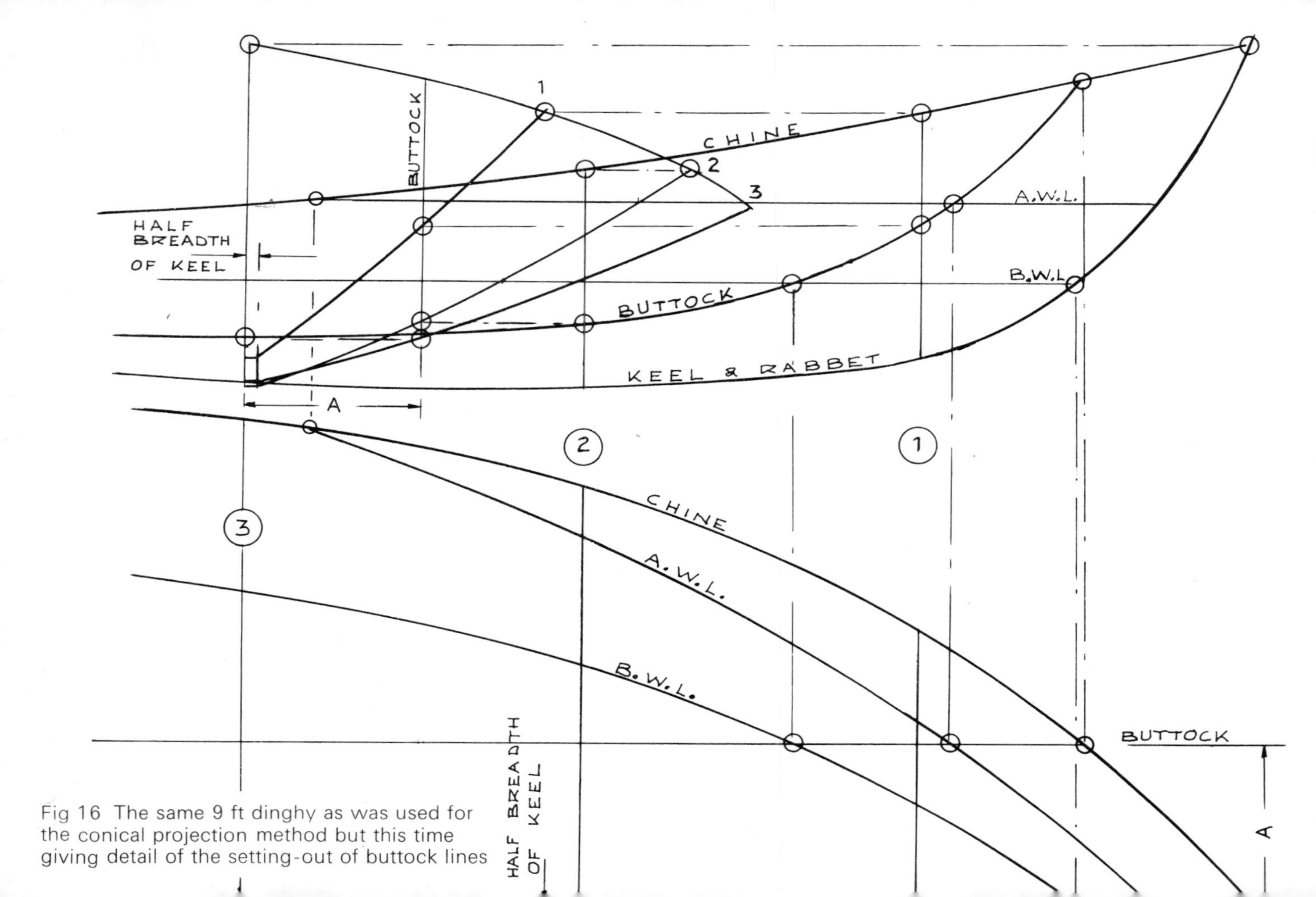

Fig 16 The same 9 ft dinghy as was used for the conical projection method but this time giving detail of the setting-out of buttock lines

same time it shows the line the ply will naturally take up at the forefoot. This helps when cutting out the bottom for the ply will nestle comfortably along the keel allowing a pencil to be wielded with speed and authority. As well as that, of course, it ensures that there is the minimum of strain on the ply and fastenings at the crucial point where the bottom and stem merge and where the ply has to follow the three diverging curves of chine, keel and stem.

As I said, you don't have to bother with this scheme and it is a bit tedious to begin with. There are other methods that can be used to predict the sectional curves but none, I think, quite so accurate at the forefoot. If steel or aluminium were the bottom sheeting material, this conic projection method, which produces a developable surface, would be of even greater importance.

Anyway, enough of the preamble. Let's get down to business and the inset sketch of fig 15 is the one to look at. A word of warning . . . since it is very difficult to predict where the various apexes will occur it is best to work on a fairly small scale lines plan to find their best positions. Having done that a bigger scale plan can be drawn shunted into whatever corner of the paper allows the apexes to be put in.

The general scheme is first to draw out the chine and keel lines (in plan and profile) as you would like them and then allow yourself small alterations of the keel in profile brought about by the projection system. These changes can generally be quite marginal provided you are prepared to spend some time shifting apexes. If you look at the examples given in the book you will get a rough idea of where to start but be prepared to alter the first shot drastically.

The Generators. The apexes must be in the same vertical line and from them draw straight lines to the intersections of chine and station lines in plan and profile. At this stage don't bother about detail but draw the lines to, say, station 0, 1 and 4, assuming a 10-station layout. The points where the generator lines (those from the two apexes) cross the rabbet in profile and the rabbet in plan must be in the same vertical line, and that inset demonstrates. Keep shifting the apexes around in any way you want, as long as they are vertically above one another, until the keel line curve in profile satisfies you. If things simply won't go right have a look at the possibility of slightly changing the slope of the chine in profile or its curve in plan. That can make quite a difference but recall all the time that you are the master and those damn lines are to serve your purpose and not the other way around.

Eventually you will hit on what looks right and then the lines to the previously omitted stations can be added and a curve drawn through the various spots given for the rabbet line in profile. It is not difficult, simply tedious. It may be necessary or wise to add a few half-stations between the existing ones forward to achieve even greater accuracy. I might add that when you become accomplished in the art of conical development it is perfectly permissible and possible to move the apexes from station to station but the method described will serve for most purposes.

This development will probably only produce results for a comparatively short length of the forebody but this is where the greatest twists occur and on transom-sterned vessels that will be enough. For the rest of the hull straight line sections will be fine. Fig 32 shows, though, how another development can be done aft for a canoe stern. The length between the developed sections can be faired in the normal way.

Waterlines. So what we have achieved thus far is a curve for the chine in plan and profile and a curve for the keel/stem in profile on to which the ply or steel will fit without trouble. Now it is necessary to take things one stage further by first determining the shape of the waterlines in plan. That inset sketch again shows the way. Two waterlines AWL and BWL are drawn on the profile view. These can, of course, be anywhere above or below LWL and must be parallel to it. Anyway, where the generator from the apex crosses the waterline in profile, drop a vertical down to hit the equivalent plan view generator. Where the two cross is the spot for the waterline in plan. Once a number of such spots have been found draw in the waterline in plan view as far as you can. The rest of it can be put in simply using the same half-breadths from the sections as was shown for LWL on fig 14. Remember the endings of all waterlines must coincide in both plan and profile.

Buttocks

These are vertical slices through the boat taken parallel to the centreline in plan view. Fig 16 vaguely demonstrates and shows the various crossing points that must coincide. Heights in section and profile must be the same and crossing points of buttocks and waterlines must be in the same vertical line in plan and profile. Note also that the distance the buttock is placed off the centreline in plan is the same as in the sectional view. Perhaps it sounds complicated but it all soon becomes second nature.

On a boat with straight line sections buttocks really need not be drawn unless you want to see what sort of shape has been arrived at, but on all curved sections such as in round-bilge vessels and conically developed hard-chine craft they are necessary to fair and smooth the lines. If we go back to the inset of fig 15 you can see how the generator lines from the apexes give the shape of the buttocks as well as of the waterlines.

Where the generators in plan cut the buttock line (which is a straight line in this view) put up a vertical to where it cuts the equivalent generator in profile. Do this on all the generators and you will have a series of spots through which a curve can be drawn and then extended aft on the method shown in fig 16. Note the endings of the buttocks on the chine and remember again that the crossing spots of waterlines and buttocks must be in the same line in profile and plan.

So, having now drawn waterlines and buttocks in plan and profile the various distances can be transferred to the sectional view. Unless you are a miraculous draughtsman there will be minor discrepancies here and there which can be faired out disregarding the marks indicated by the generators. If it had been possible to draw those with spot-on accuracy no fairing would be necessary but life is not as easy as that. If a dimension is altered on any one view it will also have to be altered in another view and these alterations may upset what has been drawn elsewhere. Don't worry, that happens all the time and all you can do is grit your teeth and carry on, never losing sight of the original curves produced by this conical development.

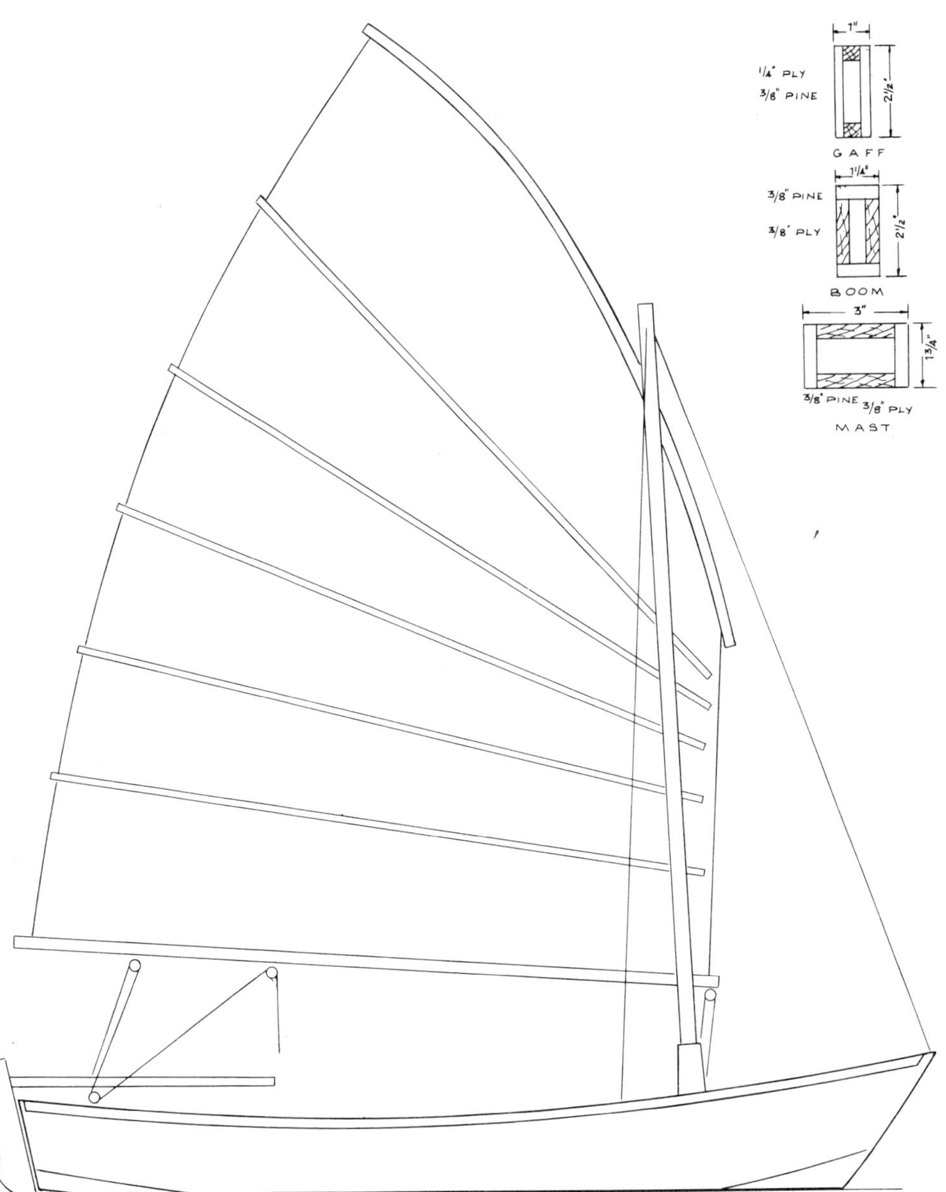

Fig 17 Profile of balanced lug sailing dinghy. LOA 15 ft 8 in. (4.77 m); LWL 12 ft 6 in. (3.81 m); beam 4 ft 6 in. (1.37 m); beam WL 4 ft (1.22 m); draught 6 in. (0.15 m); LCB 4 in. (0.1 m) fwd. of 'midships; disp. to LWL 700 lb (316 kilos); C_B 0.44; sail area 103 sq. ft (9.6 sq. m); sail area/displacement ratio when sailed single-handed 323

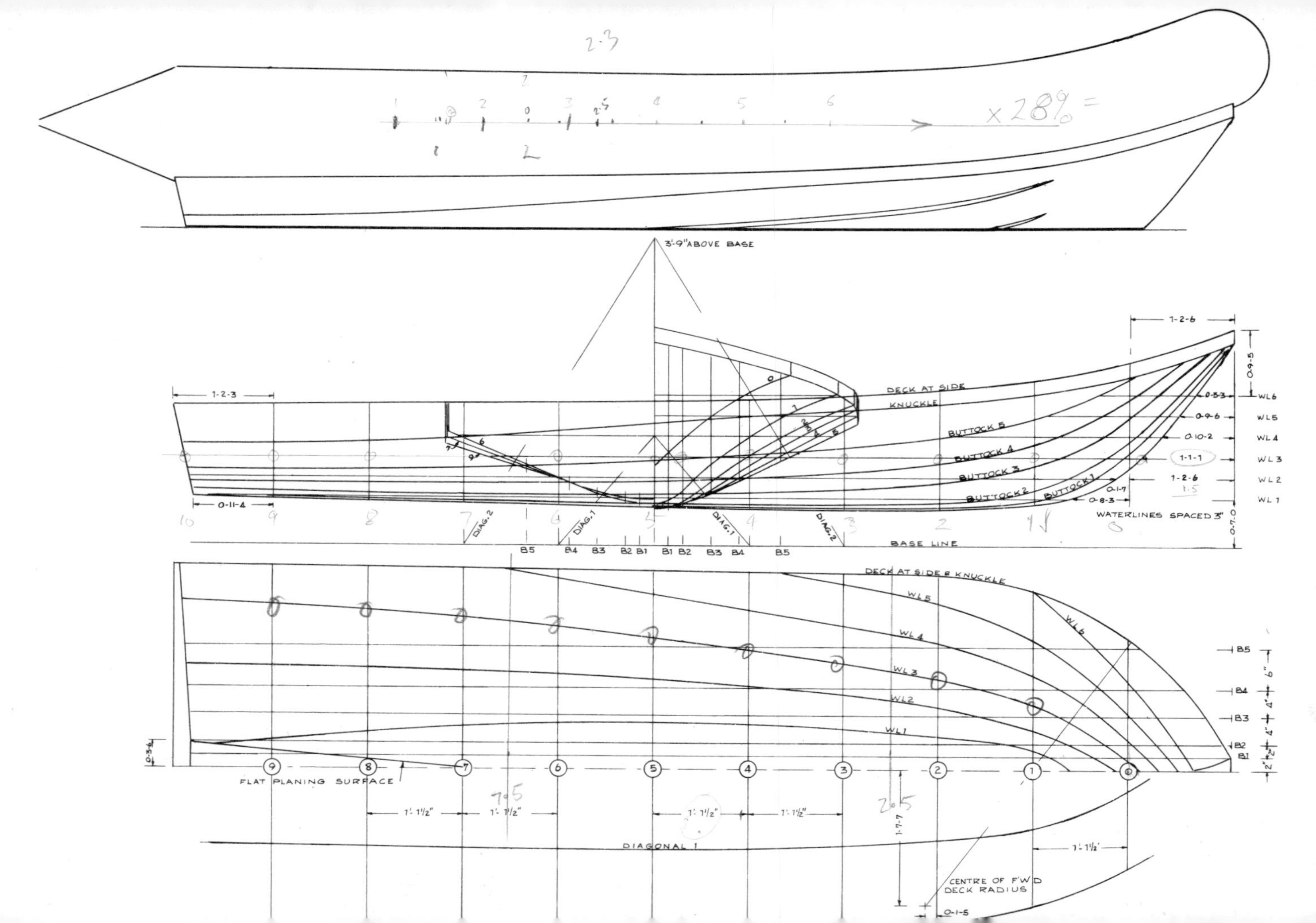
3'-9" ABOVE BASE
1-2-3
1-2-6
0-9-5
DECK AT SIDE
KNUCKLE
BUTTOCK 5
BUTTOCK 4
BUTTOCK 3
BUTTOCK 2
BUTTOCK 1
0-5-3
0-9-6
0-10-2
1-1-1
1-2-6
0-1-7
0-8-3
WL6
WL5
WL4
WL3
WL2
WL1
WATERLINES SPACED 3"
0-7-0
0-11-4
DIAG. 2
DIAG. 1
BASE LINE
B5
B4
B3
B2
B1
DECK AT SIDE & KNUCKLE
FLAT PLANING SURFACE
1'-1½"
DIAGONAL 1
1-7-7
CENTRE OF F'WD DECK RADIUS
0-1-5
0-3-6
2"
4"
6"

RIGID BOTTOM INFLATABLE

This was one of my design flops but serves to illustrate a few points and also has a curious little story attached. A few years ago I was approached by, let us call them, firm A to design the rigid bottom for a standard inflatable tube. The object of the exercise as I understood it was to produce a craft somewhat in competition with that of another concern, B, which could be used by the RNLI and similar bodies as an inshore rescue craft. By chance some time before this commission came along I had been out in some of B's craft which were of ply construction. They gave a splendid sporty ride and I much enjoyed the experience and had only one real reservation. This was that, to me anyway, it seemed as if it would be rather difficult to haul anyone from the water over the great, projecting tube. Though the transom was open it was rather cluttered up with outboards and did not appear a good alternative method of boarding.

So, I set to and drew out what you can see on fig 18. The general scheme was for a fairly conventional planing bottom with lots of curves to take advantage of the proposed G.R.P. construction. A 'flat' was worked in at the keel aft to give additional lift and, perhaps, quicker planing. It will be appreciated that a boat with a flat bottom throughout would plane more easily and more quickly than a craft with a vee in the bottom sections, though as an all-rounder it would be disastrous mainly because it would pound itself to bits in any sort of sea. A length of flat bottom aft, where pounding is unlikely to take place other than in extreme conditions, cannot be much of a disadvantage and should help speed a little.

Anyway, bearing in mind my reservations on the ease of boarding, I made a vertical wall in the sections above the waterline particularly aft, and set the tube into the hull so that it only just projected over the side. It was not such a good fender in that position and maybe I overdid it but the idea was that as people leaned over to grab someone the boat would tip quite an amount and put the tube well and truly down in the water, though it would never be submerged entirely. Then, perhaps, it would not be so difficult to heave a body over it. Of course, once the vessel was under way it would be gaining dynamical stability and would be as stable as you like.

Yes, yes, you say, and how did it work? Ah, there you have me for though I gathered that the thing had been built, that was the extent of my knowledge for quite a long time. Then, chatting to my firm A, I heard that the boat had been taken down to concern B's establishment and tested by B against their own contender. To nobody's surprise they

(*Opposite*)
Fig 18 Profile and lines plan of rigid bottom inflatable. LOA 12 ft 6½ in. (3.82 m); LWL 11 ft 3 in. (3.43 m); beam 4 ft 6 in. (1.37 m); beam WL 3 ft 3 in. (0.99 m); draught 7½ in. (0.19 m); LCB 6.65 ft (2.03 m) aft of station 0; displacement to 3WL 7451 lb (338 kilos); C_B 0.49

selected their own craft as being better and it was adopted. They had a foot in a useful door but I was a trifle annoyed! Incidents like that are not uncommon if you design for a living.

Anyway, this little boat is the only planing craft discussed in this book so we might as well now have a look at some of the criteria applicable to such boats.

Speed Prediction for Planing Craft

Remembering what speed/length ratio is, if you are designing a motor boat to do more than a speed/ratio of about 3.0 you are entering the realms of planing boats. If a mythical 25 ft waterline craft were assumed, it would be planing at $V/\sqrt{L}=3$, or $V=\sqrt{L}\times 3$
Thus, $V=\sqrt{25}\times 3=5\times 3=15$ knots.
In this case and for all higher potential speeds use the methods about to be discussed. For slower motor boats have a look at table 7 where the answers can be read straight off.

There are various methods of prediction, none of them, of course, absolutely accurate. If they were there would be far less need for tank testing but they are good enough for most purposes. Out of umpteen different formulae for the job, two have been chosen, and these are:

$$V=C\times\sqrt{\frac{BHP}{D}} \quad (1) \quad \text{and:}$$

$$V=124.7\times\frac{P^{0.551}}{W^{0.476}} \quad (2)$$

In (1), C is a constant which varies between about 3.2 for craft 20 ft on the waterline to 3.4 for 25-footers and 3.6 for 30-footers. Those constants can be extended to take in larger or smaller craft. BHP is the total brake horsepower of the engine(s) and D is displacement in tons or tonnes. An example can be worked for a 25-footer with 250 bhp installed and weighing, say 1.34 tons (3000 lb).
The sum becomes:

$$V=3.4\times\sqrt{\frac{250}{1.34}}=3.4\times\sqrt{186}=3.4\times 13.6=45.2 \text{ knots.}$$

The formula (2) was proposed by the eminent American high speed small craft specialist, Eugene Clement. In it, V is in mph, P is shaft horsepower and W is the weight, or displacement, of the boat in pounds. Shaft horsepower is the power available at the propeller shaft after going through the gearbox and so forth and can be taken as, perhaps, 10 per cent less than brake horsepower. When looking up engine catalogues for engine ratings, make sure which power is being quoted. Some manufacturers use one and some the other, while a few quote SAE powers which are not helpful though they are impressive by comparison.

So, let's work the sum again using Eugene Clement's formulae. Same boat, 25 ft on the waterline and same weight, 3000 lb. If the brake horsepower was 250, shaft horsepower would be around 225.

$$V=124.7\times\frac{225^{0.551}}{3000^{0.476}}=124.7\times\frac{19.8}{45.5}=124.7\times 0.435=54.2 \text{ mph}$$

To convert mph to knots multiply by $\frac{5280}{6080}$ so that 54.2 mph

$$\text{becomes } 54.2 \times \frac{5280}{6080} \text{ knots.}$$

That is, 47 knots. So the answers given by both formulae agree pretty well. Raising numbers to extraordinary-looking powers may strike fear in your heart but actually it is simple enough on a slide rule with a log. log. scale. If you are intending to go in for this designing business at all seriously it would be worth investing in such an instrument and studying the instructions for a few moments. Though the results are not as accurate as those produced by using log. tables or a calculator they are near enough for this type of work. A slide rule is a lot quicker than log. tables and a lot cheaper than a calculator able to perform the required manoeuvres.

That is enough on speed prediction and we might now turn our attentions briefly to general design requirements for planing boats.

Designing for Speed

We can go back to the lines of the rigid bottom inflatable now, fig 18 and the associated calculations of table 4. First it will be seen that the LCB (Longitudinal centre of buoyancy) is a 1.025 ft aft of 'midships. That means that it is 59 per cent of the waterline length aft of station 0 if you care to think of it in that way. Total waterline length is 11.25 ft, stations are spaced 1.125 ft so that station 5 is 5×1.125 ft aft of 0. That is 5.625 ft. Add the distance aft of station 5 to the LCB which was 1.025 ft and $5.625 + 1.025 = 6.65$ ft for LCB aft of 0. Percentage is then $\frac{6.65}{11.25} \times 100 = 59$ per cent. Generally speaking, the LCB and LCG should be between 55 and 60 per cent of waterline length aft of station 0 in planing craft so we are all right there.

Deadrise. Now to deadrise . . . which is the angle the bottom makes with a horizontal line through the keel. See fig 22. A flat bottom boat would have a deadrise of 0 degrees, therefore, and as has been said before, such a craft would plane easily and quickly. For practical operation, though, there must be some vee in the bottom and this can be anything between, say, 15 and 22 degrees at the transom rising to at least 45 degrees right forward. The main 'lift' point occurs round the LCG and so it is the deadrise of the bottom aft of 'midships that is most important as far as efficiency goes. The steeper the vee the less efficient but the more comfortable, at least in extreme conditions. Hence the limiting deadrise suggestions. There should not be too great a twist or change in deadrise between 'midships and the transom and if we look at this rigid-bottom inflatable we find the transom deadrise is some 17 degrees, and that at station 5 about 23 degrees. So there has been a 6 degree twist and this is about the maximum permissible for good results. It will be found that unless there is some twist it is very difficult to get a nice high chine line forward without an abrupt change in the curve of the chine in profile, which would be undesirable. Talking of profiles, maintain the keel line pretty well parallel to the LWL. Rocker in the keel can lead to high speed porpoising.

One other aspect deserves consideration. In the plan view it will be seen that the sides and chine run back parallel to the centreline so that the transom is as wide as station 5. This came about because of the shape of the tubes and is, in fact, not ideal. The transom width really ought to be about 70 per cent of maximum chine width, for this gives a rather better performance at low speeds while not detracting from it at all when the throttles are opened. If the main 'lift' occurs around the LCB and LCG then it follows that quite a bit of the aft end of the boat is not contributing much but is simply being dragged along adding only friction from its wetted surface.

Finally, on length/beam ratio; this should be about 3:1 on general purpose craft, taking chine length and chine beam as the criteria. For racing boats it can be very considerably reduced with advantage but to explain that would mean starting a discussion of trim angles and aspect ratios which need only concern designers of rather specialised vessels.

Offset Table

Before going on to one other feature of fast motor boats—their spray rails—and leaving that lines plan, fig 18, let us glance at it again. A base line is shown below the keel and offsets, or dimensions to the various useful heights of buttocks, keel, deck and knuckle will be given from that base. The widths are taken from the centreline in plan view and the whole thing is incorporated in an offset table, table 5. I think if you have a look at the thing you will see how it works. That base line can be put anywhere you like but one alternative is to measure heights above and below a particular waterline, normally LWL. Another is to assume that the baseline is the floor of the building shop and give dimensions from that. Fig 19 demonstrates what points you are dimensioning on a single chine boat, though there will actually be more waterlines and buttocks if you have done a conical development or if, as in fig 18, truly curved sections are used. From these measurements the building moulds can be made but this offset table will have to be supplemented by additional measurements at bow and stern to give the shape in profile. Fig 18 shows these. And if you had used a base line, it might as well be a sensible one allowing, say, 15 in. between the floor and the lowest point of the deck. This means that the builder can work without prostrating himself to put in the lowest row of fastenings.

Diagonals

So far waterlines and buttocks have been employed in an effort to get fair curves on the sections. However there are often spots which you will notice as you plod along with pencil and rubber where neither really ensures that the curve on one section necessarily matches up with a curve on the next. To get a final check on such areas diagonals may be drawn. What a wearisome job a lines plan is!

Again it should be said that if you have designed a craft with straight line sections none of this final fairing up will be needed. The true curves of chine, deck and rabbet are sufficient but that inflatable affair had lots of shape and would need checking. On a conical development it is hardly necessary to put in diagonals since the curves are predicted for you by the generator lines but on all round bilge boats they are used. So, here we go.

Diagonals are drawn to places where other means of fairing do not

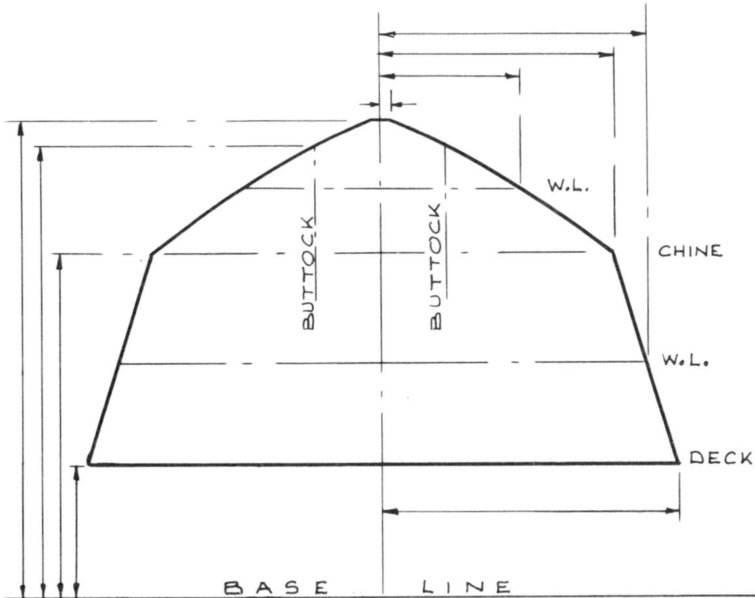

Fig 19 If a base line is drawn, offsets showing heights above it and widths from the centreline are given on the offset table for each station

seem to provide the whole answer and should be placed to cut as many stations as possible at as near right angles as possible; otherwise it doesn't matter how they are sited. Fig 20 shows a couple of possibilities. Obviously they must meet at the same point on the centreline of the sectional view and must diverge at the same angle. Don't try to measure this with a protractor but arrange the divergence by measuring out along a waterline the same distance each side. The way they are plotted is simple enough. Merely measure along the diagonal on the sectional view, or use a strip of paper with ticks on it, to the selected station and plot this measurement out from the centreline of the plan view. Repeat with all stations and draw a curve through the spots in plan. If there are discrepancies and a fair curve can't be managed, adjust the sections the appropriate amount. This adjustment will probably result in either waterlines or buttocks or both having to be adjusted also. You can merely curse and get on with it, for all such alterations were the object of the exercise.

The only awkward thing about diagonals is to know where they end and fig 20 gives examples of typical diagonals and their endings. Probably no words are necessary, simply look at the sketch.

However, to demonstrate another possibility a radiused transom has been shown and that immediately leads us into the mechanics of drawing such a thing.

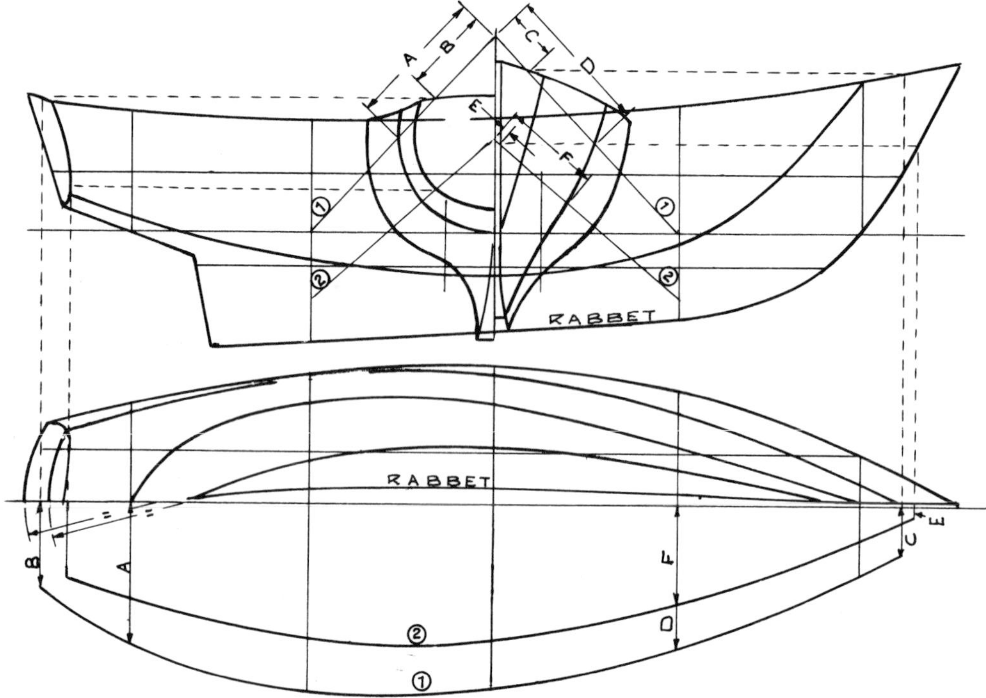

Fig 20 Because the rigid-bottom inflatable had curved sections diagonals were drawn as a check on their fairness. Here letters show some of the dimensions that must correspond when using them on another example

Radiused Transom

Fig 21 is the one to look at. What is demonstrated is how to draw a radiused transom on a lines plan, not how to develop it to its true shape in order to make the thing, which is simple enough, but we have to limit discussion somewhere. First take the compasses and draw in a transom radius, R, in plan view for the deck line. The deck at side line will cross this radius at some point and that gives one mark. Now drop a perpendicular down from the profile view where a waterline crosses the transom on the centreline, to the centreline in plan view and using the same radius as before draw another arc. Where that arc cuts the same waterline in plan view gives you another spot. This has been done on 3WL as an example. Continue with all possible waterlines.

Now turn your attention to the buttocks and on the sketch the method has been shown for B2. Where it hits the transom radius in plan, erect a vertical to where it crosses the deck at side. From this point draw a line parallel to the rake of the transom until it crosses the same buttock in profile. This gives another point and the process can be repeated for the remaining buttocks.

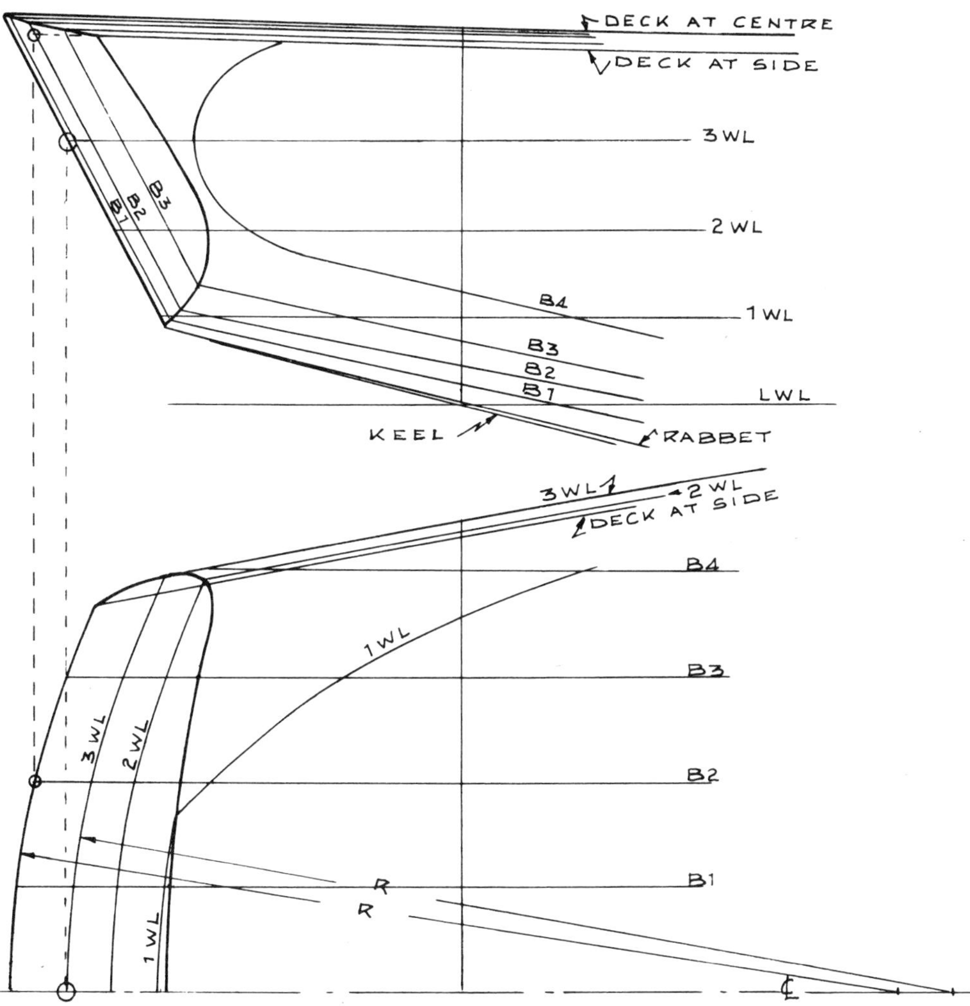

Fig 21 In conjunction with the text, this sketch shows how a radiused transom appears on a lines plan and how it is drawn

As for the deck in profile as it sweeps up the camber from the deck at side to the deck at centre, this is a tricky one to draw accurately. However, the scheme is to turn to your camber curve—described in Chapter 1—and measure out from the centreline distances corresponding to the buttock spacing. From those heights points can be marked on the buttocks in profile measured above the deck at side. Finally draw a curve through all the spots and you will have a handsome shape, though one that is actually not a lot of use except to satisfy your aesthetic sensibilities.

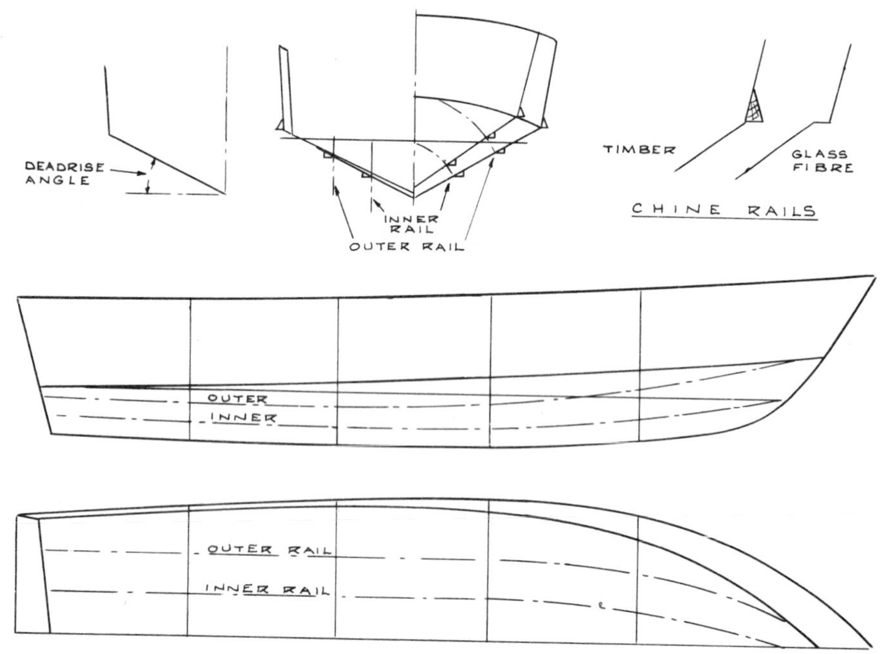

Fig 22 Because water does not flow in straight lines, particularly forward, spray rails forward should show a gentle curve and not follow buttock lines. The left-hand sketch demonstrates what is meant by deadrise angle, which is also called rise of floor

Spray Rails

Having sorted out the strange bits of the lines plan for the rigid-bottom inflatable we could have a last look at the craft and ponder about spray rails. It had two per side, as can be perceived on fig 23. These things, whatever their merits, are mounted by popular demand on just about every fast motor boat.

Generally speaking, their principal use is, as their name implies, to deflect spray away from the boat and thus reduce the wetted surface and in flattish-floored boats up to, say, 15 degrees deadrise at 'midships they do nothing else. Hence they should only run from about 'midships to the point forward where they become hard to fit due to the rapidly changing shape of the boat. Bottom surfaces of the rails should be parallel to the waterline and width can be quite moderate. Something like 3 in. would be fine for a 25-footer, scaled up or down according to actual boat length. On G.R.P. construction they are incorporated with the hull moulding. On timber craft they are additions.

Besides these bottom strakes it is most important to have a spray rail the whole length of the vessel at the chine and fig 22 shows this. Without it water will run up the sides at speed and increase resistance considerably.

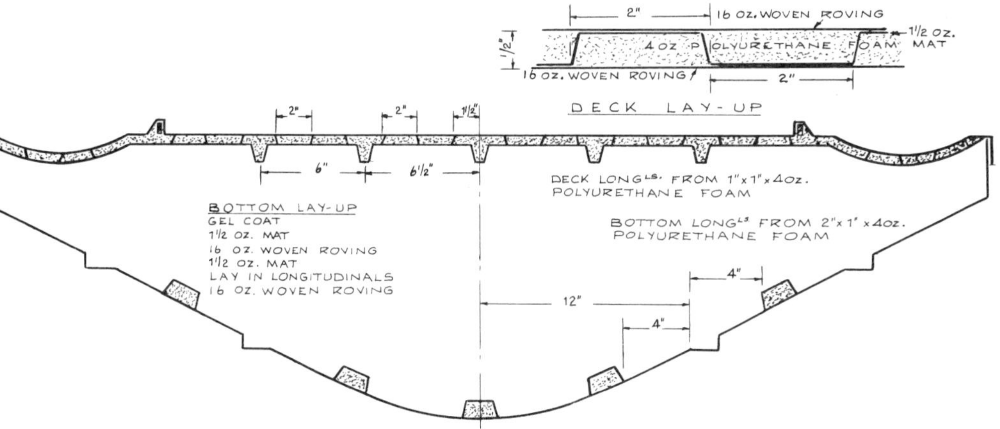

Fig 23 Structural section of the rigid-bottom inflatable

On really fast, steeply vee'd craft bottom rails play an additional role in that they define the boat's beam at high speed. As the vessel rises in the water with throttles opened strategically placed spray rails each side may confine the water to the width between them. This again reduces wetted surface but also effectively diminishes the beam of the craft which can be an advantage at very high speeds. Since it is impossible to predict to what height the boat will rise two or three sets of rails will have to be slung along the bottom in the fair hope that one set will do the trick.

Spray rails run along buttocks lines aft from 'midships but forward should curve in towards the bow in a gentle arc. Fig 22 shows the sort of thing to aim for.

Glassfibre Construction

This little inflatable affair is built of G.R.P.—that is glassfibre plus polyester resin—and it is probably worth including a dissertation on the basic outline of this form of construction. Anyone wanting to tackle the job properly should get hold of Lloyds' Rules for the Construction of Reinforced Plastic Yachts or the equivalent publication from Norske Veritas. These go into far more details of scantlings, framing methods and so on than is possible here. F.R.P. Design Data published by Fibreglass Limited is also valuable as is Scott Bader's Polyester Handbook.

The figures that apply to this section are 23, 24, 25 and 26 and we can start with fig 24. This gives an idea, first, of shell weight for various lengths of craft; second, stiffener spacing required with that shell weight (but not stiffener size for which you will have to make a guess if not working with Lloyds at your elbow); and, third, the stiffness of solid G.R.P. compared with a foam sandwich construction.

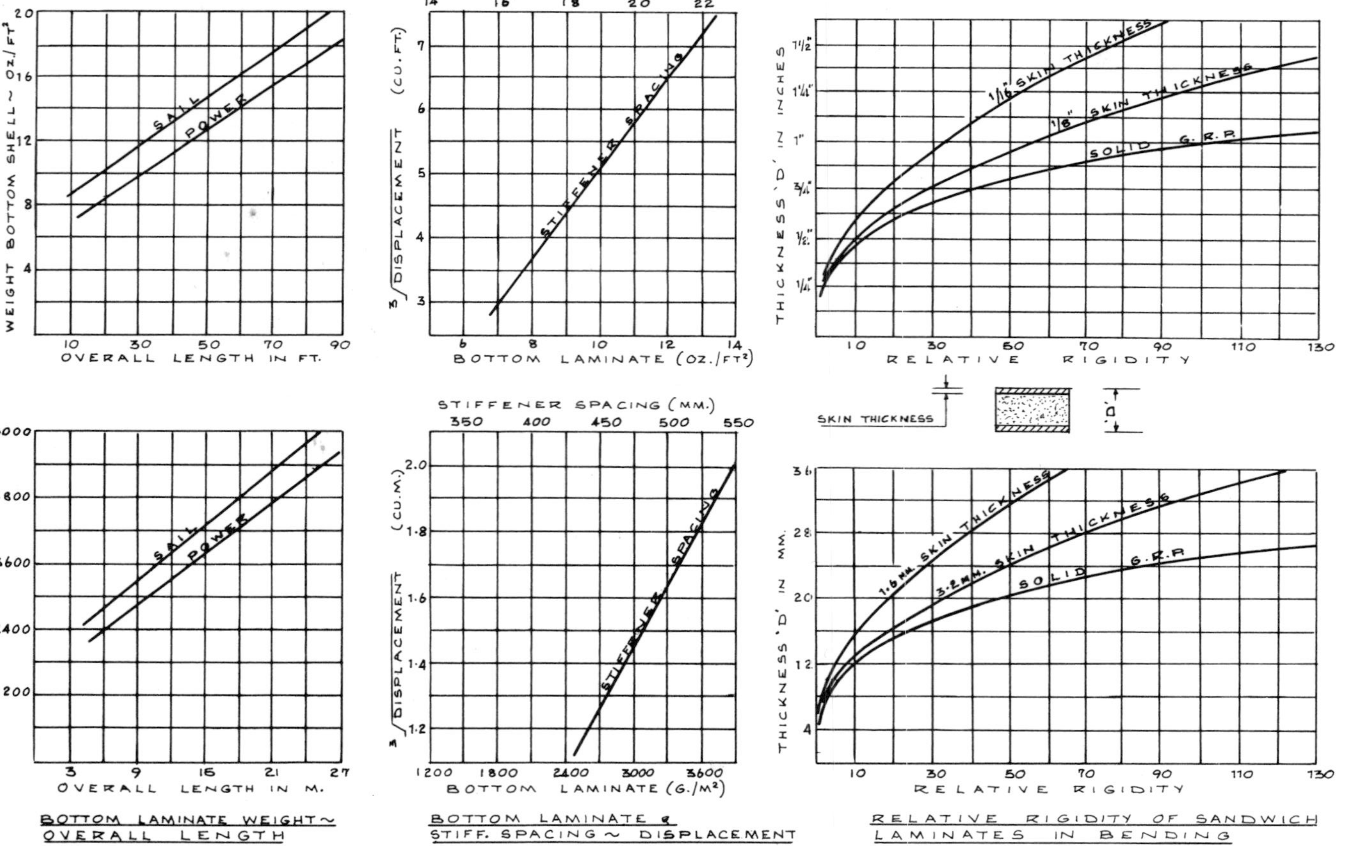

Fig 24 With these graphs G.R.P. hull weights and stiffener spacing can be determined with reasonable accuracy for different lengths of boat. Also an idea of the size and type of foam sandwich construction of equivalent strength to solid G.R.P. can be gained

Fig 25 Some details of typical G.R.P. construction

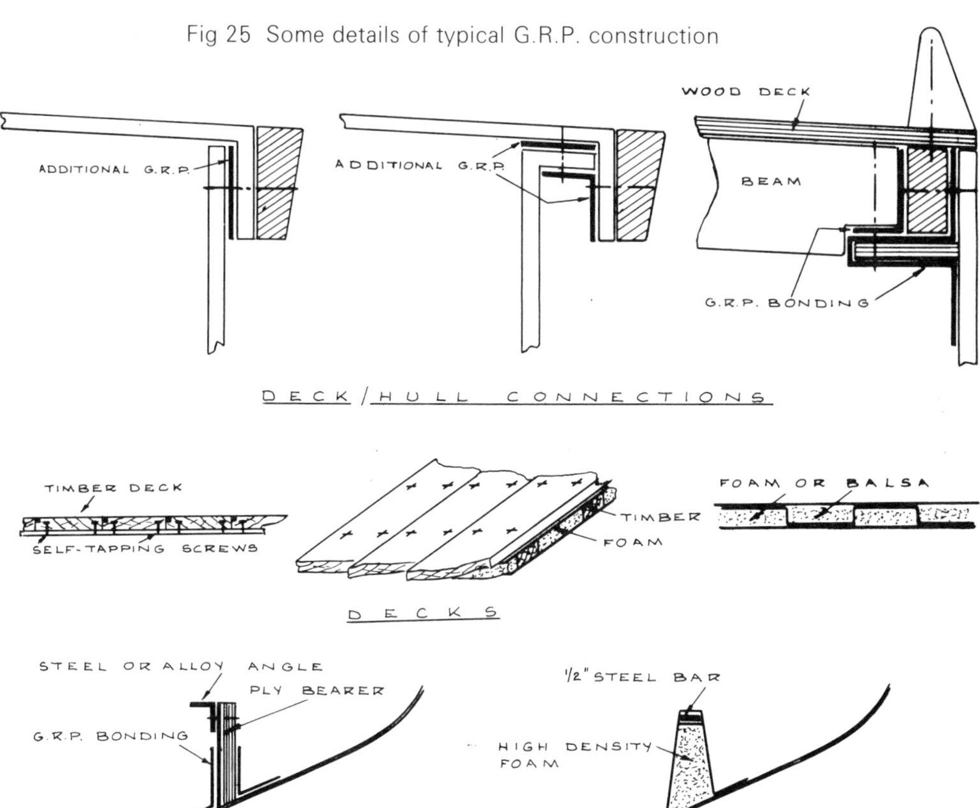

The left-hand graph is easy enough to follow. If your designed boat were 25 ft in length and intended to sail, the shell weight should be around 11 oz/sq. ft. This sort of laminate can be achieved in various ways. The simplest would be to use all chopped strand mat which comes, basically, in 1 oz, 1½ oz and 2 oz/sq. ft varieties. It is the cheapest of all usable glassfibre types and wets-out easily. In other words it is no problem to work the resin through the glass so that it bonds happily with the preceding layer. The graph we have just looked at assumes an all-chopped strand mat lay-up (as do Lloyds in their Rules) so there should be adequate strength.

Weight of Final Laminate. In this case the resin/glass ratio will probably be quite close to 3:1. That is for each ounce of glass 3 oz of resin will have to be used to bind everything together. It follows then that each layer of one ounce mat will actually weigh four ounces as used on the boat and our suggested 11 oz lay-up for this 25-footer will weigh $11 + (3 \times 11) = 11 + 33 = 44$ oz per square foot, allowing for resin.

Exactly the same reasoning applies when using metric weights in the bottom left-hand graph. Chopped strand mat is generally available in 300, 450 and 600 grams/sq. metre weights and the final laminate will come out at something like four times the weight of glass alone.

By careful supervision and with kits of appropriate amounts of glass and resin good laminators can reduce the resin/glass ratio to about $2\frac{1}{2}:1$ and even 2:1 if woven rovings are used in place of mat in the lay-up. This has two advantages. The first being that the higher proportion of glass to resin, the stronger the final laminate. Secondly, woven rovings are themselves stronger than mat, though they are more difficult to wet-out. Because of this a layer of mat should be placed between each layer of rovings. This has been done on the rigid-bottom inflatable and fig 23 shows a structural section. The note to the effect that the longitudinals are laid in just before the final layer of rovings simply means that the foam cores of these longitudinals are positioned just before the final layer, which then covers everything. That boat is about 12 ft long overall and according to the graph of fig 24 would require about $7\frac{1}{2}$ oz of glass on its shell. Woven roving weights are given in ounces per square yard, not per square foot, by the makers and so you can see that the weight is (if we take the 16 oz rovings as being 1.75 oz/sq. ft) $1.5+1.75+1.5+1.75=6.5$ oz/sq. ft. Since we have used some rovings and not mat exclusively that should be satisfactory. The gel coat, incidentally, is the layer of special flexible resin that is applied to the outside of the laminate. It is waterproof and resiliant. A normal laminate will draw water up the strands of glass and this can cause trouble, so the outer gel coat is vital. Too low a proportion of resin to glass, whatever its strength, has poor weathering properties and would not last for long on a boat. Those ratios indicated are satisfactory.

Stiffener Spacing. Now we could have a look at the middle of the three sets of graphs of fig 24. These show stiffener spacing and the stiffeners may run transversely or longitudinally—it doesn't matter which. The only proviso here is that if you opted for longitudinal framing, which is in many ways the best, and found that the recommended spacing was, say 20 in., at every five times that spacing there should be a transverse frame. Thus, you would want longitudinals at 20 in. and a transverse every 100 in. This requirement is normally automatically catered for by bulkheads, moulded-in seats and so forth which occur as part of the boat's function.

Anyway, for this middle graph we are dealing in displacement volume rather than weight. Table 4 shows the calculation for two craft. The first is the inflatable again.

$$\text{Displacement weight} = 745 \text{ lb so displacement volume} = \frac{745}{64}$$

$$= 11.6 \text{ cu. ft}$$

The second example is actually for a 40 ft (12.19 m) sailing boat.

Displacement weight 9300 kilos = 9.3 cu. m.

The cube root of 11.6 is 2.26 so if we look at the top, middle graph we find that stiffeners should be spaced at about 15 in. and that the bottom shell, as a check on the previous result, should be about $6\frac{1}{2}$ oz/sq. ft.

For the bigger yacht, the cube root of 9.3 is 2.2 and so the stiffener spacing should be about 550 mm and the bottom laminate around 4000 g/sq. m. In fact on the actual boat the bottom was 5000 g reducing to some 4250 g on the topsides and the stiffeners were as recommended.

As mentioned, this approximate scantling selection method does not give actual framing sizes and you will just have to make an arbitrary guess bearing in mind that the more the skin thickness is increased over the recommended the smaller can be the stiffeners, though putting all the weight in the shell tends to be rather expensive.

Should you be working out a weight calculation for G.R.P. construction, a guide is that the weight of the framing will be about one-third of the shell.

Foam Sandwich. The right hand graphs of this figure compare stiffness of a foam sandwich construction with that of solid G.R.P. The strength of the foam, which would normally be an expanded polyurethane (such as Bulstrode Tuf-foam at 5 lb/cu. ft) for hard chine craft whether with developed surfaces or not or an expanded P.V.C. foam of around the same weight (Airex or Plasticell) for round bilge boats where ease of bending is important, is not a significant factor here.

Looking at the curves it will be seen that if, for instance, solid glassfibre $\frac{3}{4}$ in. thick were used it could be replaced by a sandwich about $\frac{7}{8}$ in. thick complete with $\frac{1}{8}$ in. glass each side of the foam or by a sandwich nearly $1\frac{1}{8}$ in. total thickness with two $\frac{1}{16}$ in. layers of glass. All these have the same relative rigidity values. To give an idea of what this means in practice, a one ounce G.R.P. laminate (this is the weight of the glass and assumes appropriate resin) is about $\frac{1}{32}$ in. thick, while a 300 g laminate is 1 mm thick or near enough. Thus, say if you were using a 10 oz lay-up, thickness would be $\frac{10}{32}$ in., or $\frac{5}{16}$ in. while a 4500 g laminate would be $\frac{4500}{300}$ or 15 mm in thickness.

If you ponder that and consider the shell construction recommended for the two craft already discussed it will be borne on you that there is not going to be very much advantage in using a foam sandwich for the hull. A small amount of weight will be saved but not as much as you might have hoped as the outer layer of glassfibre will almost certainly have to be thicker than that suggested by the curves in order to resist abrasion. It would hardly be practical to use a boat with only $\frac{1}{16}$ in. of glassfibre on the bottom. The first unintentional grounding would quite probably tear a hole in the stuff.

Decks. So, for the size of craft considered in this book sandwich construction for hulls is employed either to gain a much stiffer hull than would be given by solid G.R.P., though with little weight saving, or to avoid the use of an expensive mould. When employing foam it can be laid up over a simple batten mould, as is explained in Chapter 4. For decks the stiffness of a G.R.P. sandwich is of greater advantage. In solid G.R.P. decks are normally around the same thickness as the shell and on small craft this often leads to a very bouncy structure. It may be strong enough but it certainly doesn't feel it. So a sandwich is used instead, as on the little inflatable of fig 23. One feature may need a little explanation there. Though foam cores are strong enough in compression they tend to have a rather low resistance to shearing forces and can fail under sudden strains. Therefore it is wise to use the glassfibre to form webs and to break up the foam in smallish panels. The same applies to hulls and one way to do it is shown in the dinghy of Chapter 4.

Construction Details. Fig 25 shows a few details of G.R.P. construction. The top sketches concern themselves with hull/deck connections. The left-hand illustration shows the neatest way of doing the job but one which requires a very accurate deck moulding which must be a snug fit all the way round the hull. The centre method is more tolerant of discrepancies between the two mouldings, while the right-hand side sketch shows one way to fasten a wood deck to a G.R.P. hull. The deck beams sit on a timber beam shelf glassed to the hull.

The middle line of drawings deals with decks only. On the left a timber deck is fastened to a G.R.P. deck with self-tapping screws and there should be a layer of mastic or wet glassfibre between the two. In the middle it is presumed that a wooden deck is to be fastened to a foam sandwich deck. To do this there are alternate layers of timber and foam in the sandwich so as to give something in which to fasten screws from the top timber structure. On the right the method of breaking up the foam core and using glassfibre as webs is shown again in a sort of stylised version. Note that end-grain balsa wood can be employed in place of foam. It is more expensive but is strong and the resin from the laminate gets a really good grip on the end grain so that de-lamination between the outer skins and core is most unlikely. That can happen with a foam core.

Along the bottom two ways of building engine beds in a G.R.P. hull are shown. Both are perfectly satisfactory though the left-hand scheme is the more common. By high-density foam is meant something about 18–20 lb/cu. ft.

16 ft CATAMARAN

And now for something entirely different. When we build a boat at home we usually try and turn out something a bit out of the ordinary, partly for interest's sake and partly to see how it works. But since a boat costs money even if you knock it up in the back garden we have to try and justify this expense somehow and employ all manner of rather feeble arguments to this end. In the case of the catamaran I deluded myself that there was a market for a smallish camping boat which would not be tied to one particular function. That is, it should be capable of being used to tow a water ski-er as well as under sail or small outboard. It had to be simple to build, of course. Once completed and tested we would be able to sell plans like hot cakes and retire on the proceeds. Like all our similar ideas, though, it went off at half-cock for having built the boat we were much more interested in using it than seeking publicity and doing all the hard work necessary to get the thing before the public's gaze.

Fig 26 Catamaran profile. LOA 15 ft 7 in. (4.75 m); LWL 14 ft 3 in. (4.34 m); beam overall 7 ft 4 in. (2.24 m); hull beam each 2 ft (0.61 m); draught $7\frac{1}{2}$ in. (0.19 m); LCB 8.84 ft (2.7 m) aft of station 0; displacement to LWL 460 lb (208 kilos); C_B (each hull) 0.2; sail area 132 sq. ft (12.1 sq. m); sail area/displacement ratio 274 (at 750 lb (340 kilos) displacement)

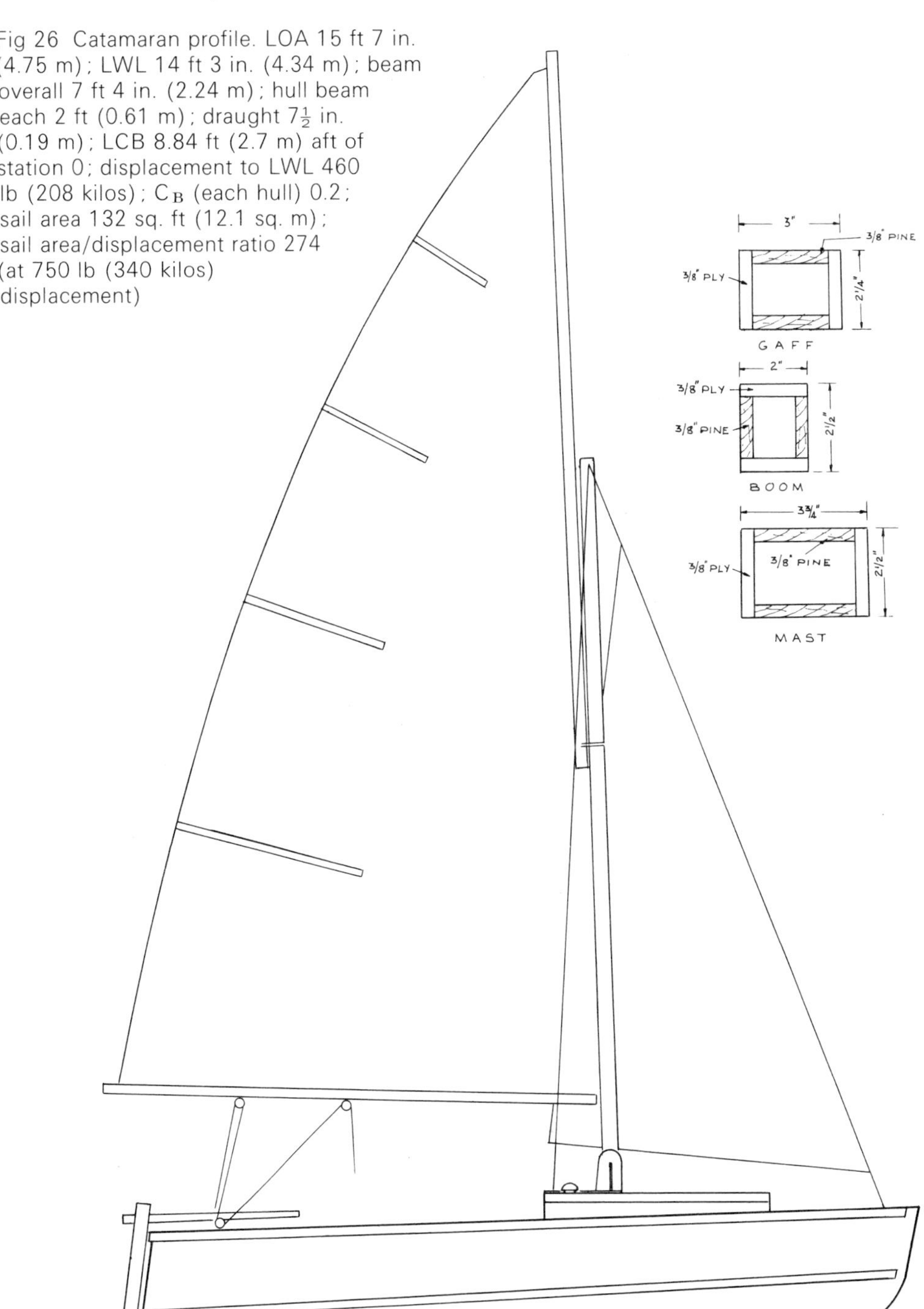

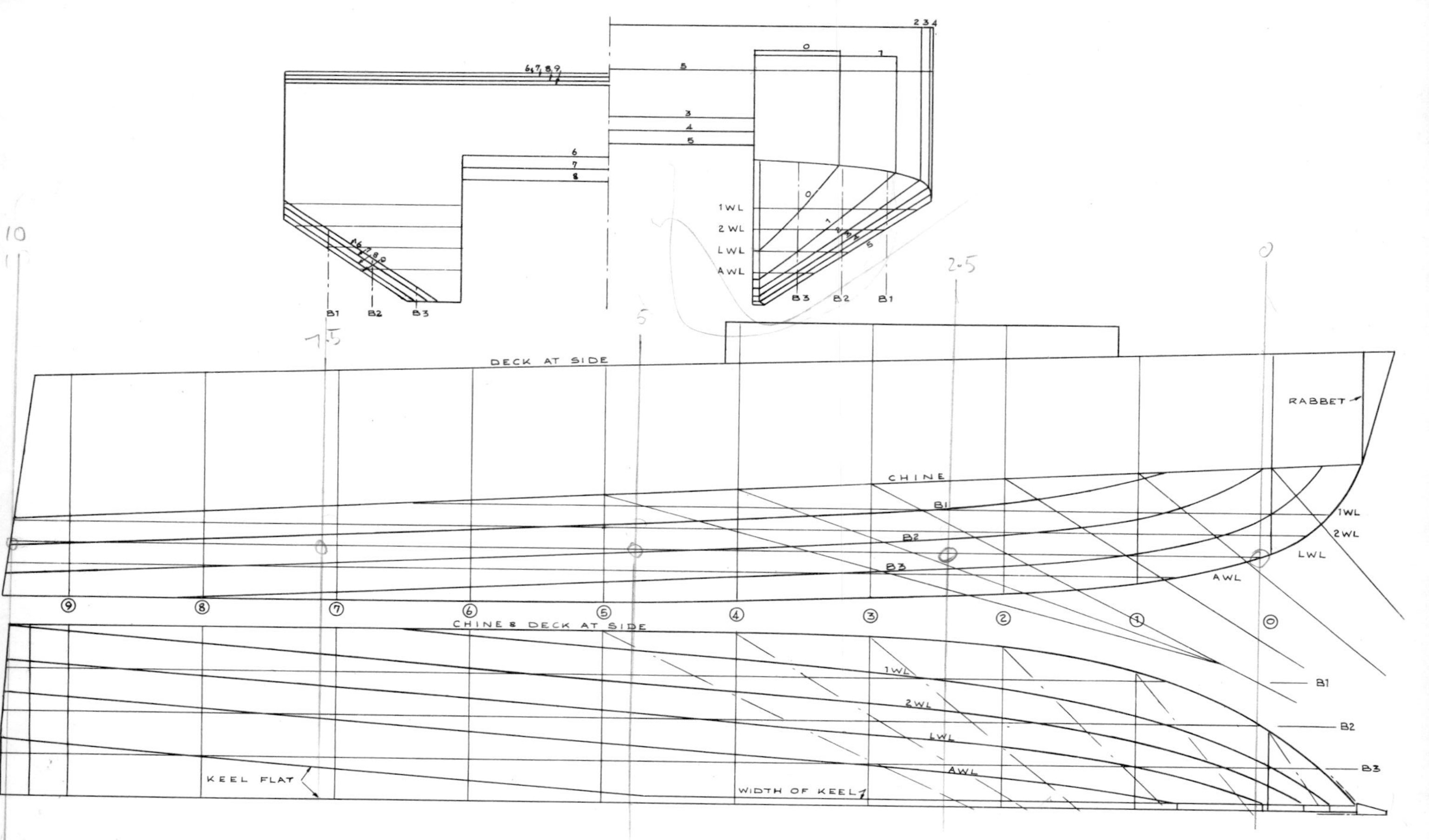

Fig 27 The lines of the catamaran are unusual in that the buttocks slope down throughout their length. The excuse for that is given in the text but the boat still seems to sail well enough

Generally speaking, craft with a power boat planing performance are pretty useless under sail because of the wide, deeply immersed transom necessary for genuine speed with an engine. The only possible exception seemed to be a catamaran which, though immersed transoms would still be necessary, could have them on comparatively narrow hulls with the result that their submerged area would be less than on a conventional form. If a catamaran has narrow hulls and is not built as a lightweight racing machine those hulls are necessarily fairly deeply immersed to give a potentially better performance under sail than a conventional craft with less draught. And a catamaran has an enormous amount of initial stability which might encourage those who normally motored or water-skied to have a shot at sailing.

Finally, the great overall beam of a cat. makes the planning of primitive accommodation easy. In fact we can sleep four on this boat without trouble; one in each 'cabin' and two on the bridge deck. Cabin is something of a misnomer since one has to insinuate oneself feet first straight into a sleeping bag but once installed it is comfortable enough. We have a boom tent which is put up at night and under which there is headroom for cooking and so forth.

In action we are happy with the boat. Though the lines are slightly odd—the reason for this will be discussed in a minute—she sails quite well and will go to windward in even a light breeze provided one is satisfied with stately rather than electrifying performance. Generally the jib has to be backed to get the head round and in rough water it is sometimes necessary to gybe or at least to bear off and get up some

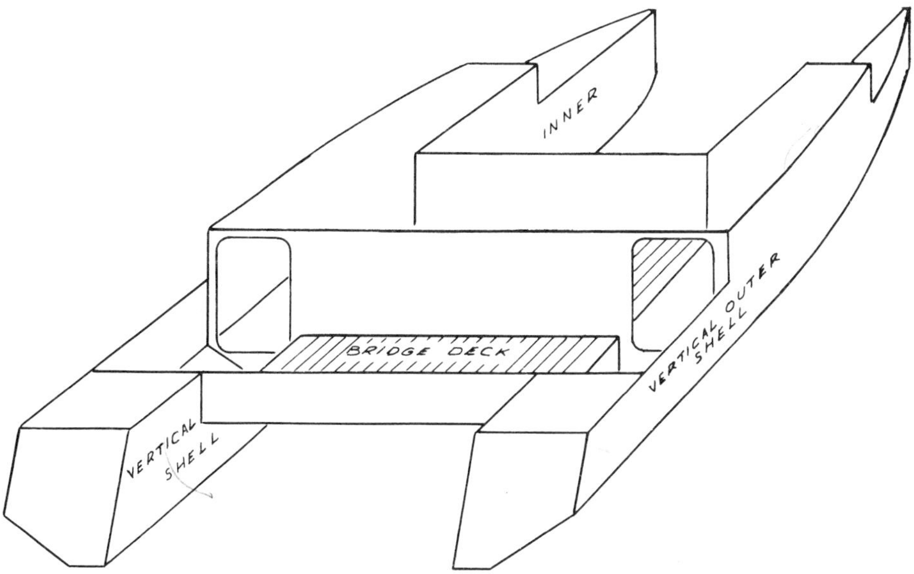

Fig 28 The structural scheme for the catamaran which allowed us to prefabricate much of the structure

real speed before attempting to swing through the wind.

Performance under Power. We have a Seagull Silver Century outboard which propels the craft in a workmanlike manner. We once borrowed a 25 hp outboard to see what happened and with an eye to water ski-ing. Unhappily the propeller pitch was too coarse for we could not coax the thing above 4000 rpm as against its maximum of 5500, so power was well down. It gave a fraction over 12 knots with four aboard but the fuel consumption was so frightening—we are not used to anything over 4 hp—that we abandoned the experiment. It was found, though, that

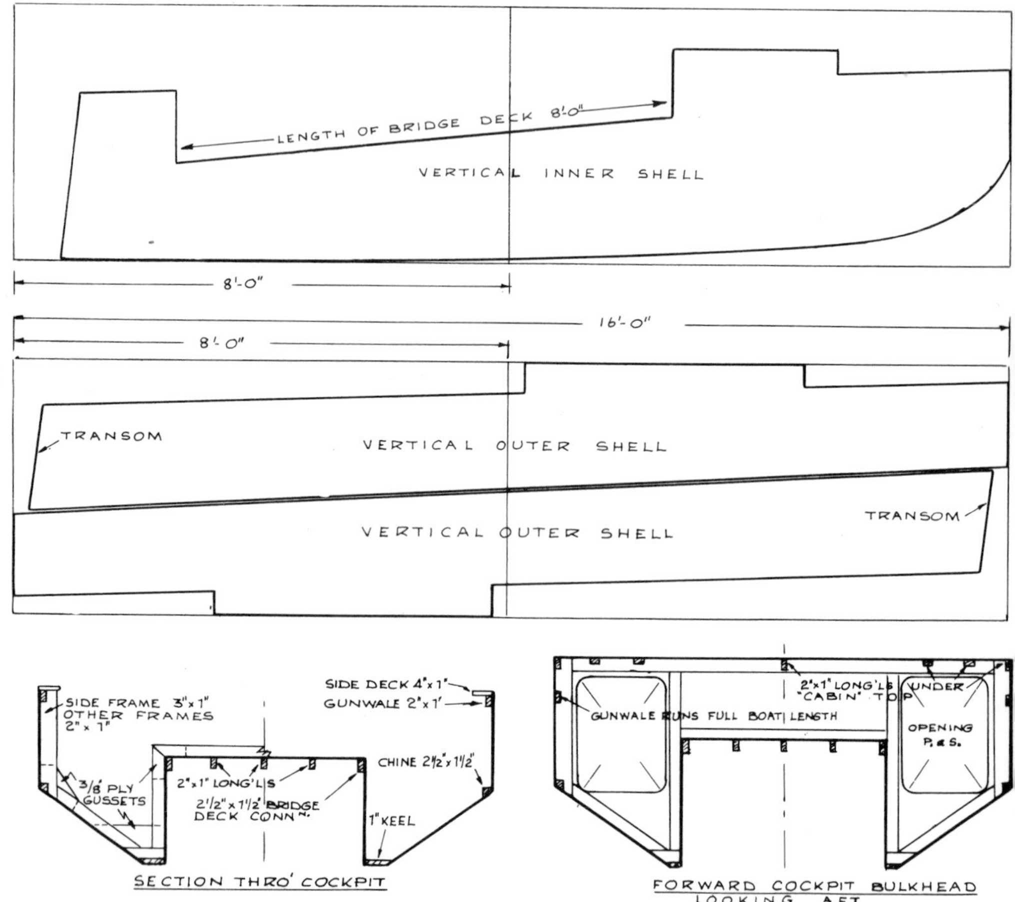

Fig 29 To quite a large extent the shape of the cat was dictated by the most economical use of ply. The topside framing was wider than the bottom framing because it gave better holding for the screws through the chine. In any case 9 mm ply is enormously rigid when given a bit of a twist and framing on this size and form of boat is largely superfluous

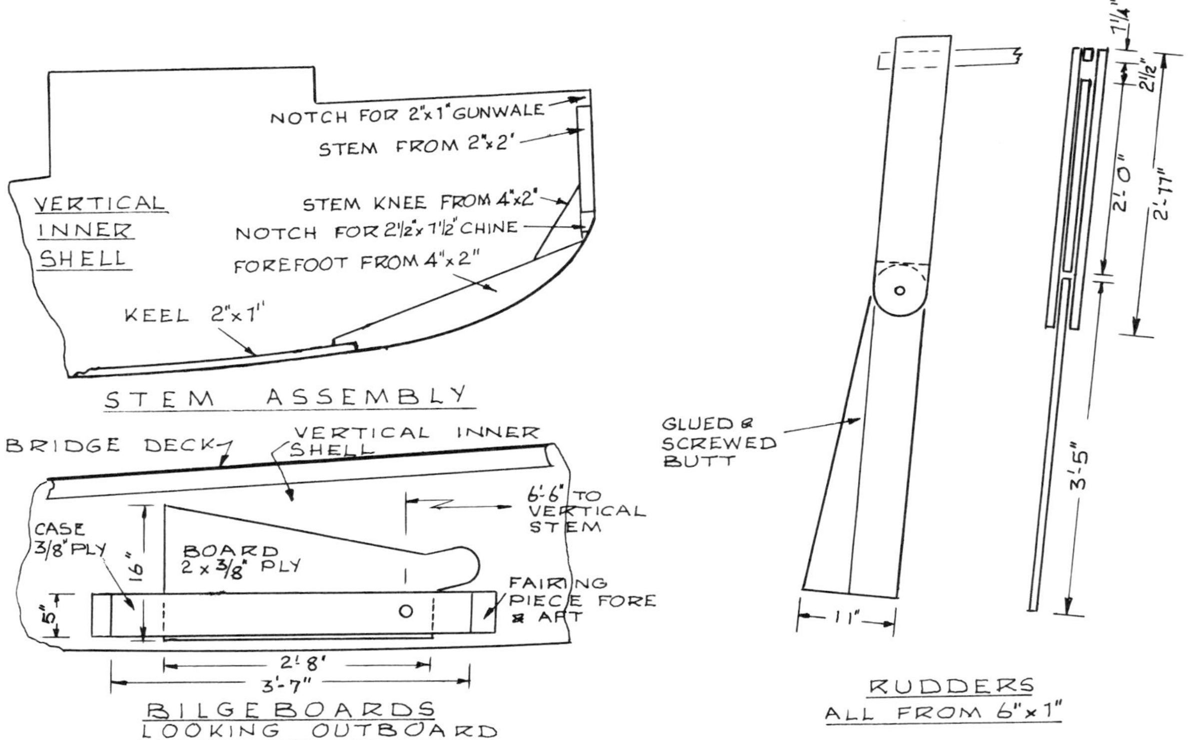

Fig 30 The cat rudders, bilge boards and stem assembly

with the motor mounted between the hulls at the aft end of the bridge deck, which ends some 3 ft forward of the transoms, attempting sharp turns resulted in stupendous cavitation for the propeller was unable to draw in proper supplies of water, being masked by the hulls. Clearly the bridge deck would have to be extended right to the stern if powerful outboards were to be used.

Construction. Anyway, figs 26–30 apply here and we might as well go straight to figs 28 and 29 which show vaguely how the boat was put together and in some way explain one or two features of the lines plan (fig 27). Once again the idea was to be able to construct the craft without the use of building moulds and the basis of the scheme was the two vertical and straight inner hulls. Clearly their shape could be found directly from a drawing. They were kept at the correct distance apart by a straight-sided bridge deck and had bulkheads and frames fastened to and slotted over them. To these were fastened the vertical outer shells. Though there was a curve in these as they ran in towards the bow, that curve could be expanded into a straight line with the result that these, too, could be marked and cut out direct from a drawing. To save material, both outer shells were cut from two sheets of ply laid end to end, fig 29, and as these sides also incorporated the 'cabin' sides this governed the overall height. The sheer was a straight line, as was the chine, and one ended up with a pile of wood which could be rapidly assembled. The only things that required marking out on the job were the two bottoms and since they butted into a straight chine line and the sections were conically developed to give an easy curve to the forefoot that was a simple task. Decks and cabin tops were straight—no camber—and using $\frac{3}{8}$ in (9 mm) ply for everything they were adequately stiff with a minimum of framing.

With that behind us the lines plan, fig 27, may not be quite so strange. Though bevelling chines and keels is not quite such a fearsome job as it would seem, a constantly changing bevel certainly needs a reasonable amount of care and attention to get it right. If this work could be reduced, so much the better, so the sections from about station 4 (where the curve to the bow ends) to the stern had a constant deadrise. This would mean that since the inner and outer shells were parallel, the keel would run down parallel to the chine and give an enormously deep hull aft. To overcome that we made a flat keel growing gradually wider as it went aft so as to keep it parallel to the waterlines. This did not affect the constant bevel angle and since the keel was merely made of a length of plank and could be marked out from the drawings it was simple enough to construct.

Buttock Lines. The result of all this was, as will be seen, that the buttocks run downhill all the way. I wondered how this would affect sailing performance and whether it might even help in directing the flow of water clear of the transom at high speeds. Whether it does or not I can't say, since I have forgotten to look at the appropriate times. The sloping buttock lines would be dangerous at very high velocities as the boat, like all boats, would tend to trim such that the buttocks were flat on the water and this would induce a dreadful nose-down trim. But at normal operating speeds and even when water ski-ing that shouldn't happen.

Trapezoidal System for Displacement

There is plenty of flare to the bottom itself so that the craft is comparatively dry but the rather strange shape has brought the LCB a long way aft. Table 6 shows the displacement and LCB calculation as well as the calculation for the position of the longitudinal centre of gravity (LCG).

The displacement has been worked using the trapezoidal system. I have assumed that station 9 marks the end of the waterline, which it doesn't but the length overhanging won't make much difference to the final answer. With this scheme the area of each submerged section is first found. We have actually taken the loaded waterline as 2WL here. LWL is the waterline of the boat complete but without anything aboard.

The areas are jotted down opposite the stations and the totals then taken. The total of the first and last numbers (stations 0 and 9 in this case) are divided by two and added to the total of all other areas. This number is multiplied by two, since there are two hulls, and by the spacing between the stations. In this case the spacing was 1.5 ft. The answer is in cu. ft or cubic anything else, depending on how you have measured the areas. So far so good.

Centre of Buoyancy. Next we need the LCB and this has been done in a rather similar manner to that employed for the other three examples of tables 1 and 4. Select any station you like and multiply the distance the areas are away from that station. Station 3 is 1.5 ft from station 4, for example, and station 7, 3×1.5 ft $= 4.5$ ft from station 4. Add the totals as shown, take the smaller from the larger and divide that number by the grand total of the areas.

Well, we find from that the LCB is 8.84 ft from station 0 which is a long way past 'midships and doubts must arise as to how the LCG of hull and equipment compare.

Table 6 shows how to find this out. Put down all the bits of hull structure, the weight of each and what you judge to be its LCG from a certain point. Station 0 has been chosen as that point here. Add the weights; multiply the distances by the weights and add their totals. Allow a further one third of the total weight for framing and bits you have forgotten and give it the same LCG as the previous answer. Multiply weight by distance again and add those two totals. Now do the same thing for bits of equipment and arrange storage spaces, at least mentally, for as many of these items as far aft as you can get them for we have to try and balance the boat over the LCB. Finally add the three totals and divide the moments column (weight times distance) by the weights column. Forget the crew for they can seat themselves as they want and will, in any case, be shifting about. The calculated weight of 713 lb is 37 lb less than the assumed displacement of 750 lb, but that is really near enough.

Moment to Change Trim

It appears that our LCG, not counting the crew, is 0.64 ft forward of the LCB. In the calculations we have been quite moderate on weight estimations but it looks as if we are stuck with that figure. What will its effect be? Well, we can estimate that by using a formula called Moment to Change Trim lin, or MCT.

$$\text{MCT} = \frac{\text{Displacement}}{10}$$

In this case the displacement was 750 lb: $MCT = \frac{750}{10} = 75$

This means that if you shifted 75 lb one foot in distance it would change the trim of the boat by 1 in. We have effectively shifted 713 lb a distance of 0.64 ft. Multiplied that implies that we have shifted $713 \times 0.64 = 456$ lb one foot. Thus the boat will trim by $456/75 = 6.2$ in. Trim will be by the bow in this case since our LCG was forward of the LCB. Though not precisely accurate, you can say that half that trim will occur forward and half aft. That is the boat will float 3 in. deep at the bow and 3 in. high at the stern.

If you feel masochistic that waterline can be drawn on the plan so that you can see what the result will look like. On the catamaran it means that the chine and deck look to be parallel to the waterline—though I know they can't both be! Of course once aboard, a crew of two or three or four soon right things since the man at the helm must sit right aft and if someone is handling the sheet he is fairly well forced to sit aft too. Galley stores are kept in the aft locker so anyone wanting to brew up comes aft—it is a good thing we have a beam of 7 ft 4 in. and there is acres of space in the cockpit. Anyway, she seems to trim right in sailing conditions, which is what is wanted. It is no use having a craft sitting beautifully trimmed at moorings only to have the whole thing spoiled as soon as the crew come along and take up their normal positions.

3. Double Chine Forms

By having two chines per side rather than one a boat can get quite near the clean lines and efficiency of a true round bilge hull but it is senseless to continue multiplying chines indefinitely. Unless there are urgent reasons for using a sheet material in a straightforward manner—an example might be an amateur building in steel who didn't feel capable of forming the compound curves demanded by a round bilge—two chines are really the practical limit above which it is usually easier to construct a normal round bottom form. The resulting vessel can be attractive to look at especially if the upper chine is kept above the load waterline throughout its length, for in many conditions a shadow is thrown below that chine which helps to reduce any potentially slab-sided look. Sharp angles in sections dampen rolling and throw spray clear of the sides, lessening wetted surface, apart from creating a drier boat. Generally speaking, too, a chine form will have a slightly better performance under power than round bilge especially at speeds above a speed/length ratio of 1. So all in all the double chine isn't a bad shape at all.

Anyone who has got this far in the book and understands the job of fairing the lines and which points must correspond in the various views will have no trouble in drawing a double chine boat and so we might as well plunge straight into the first example.

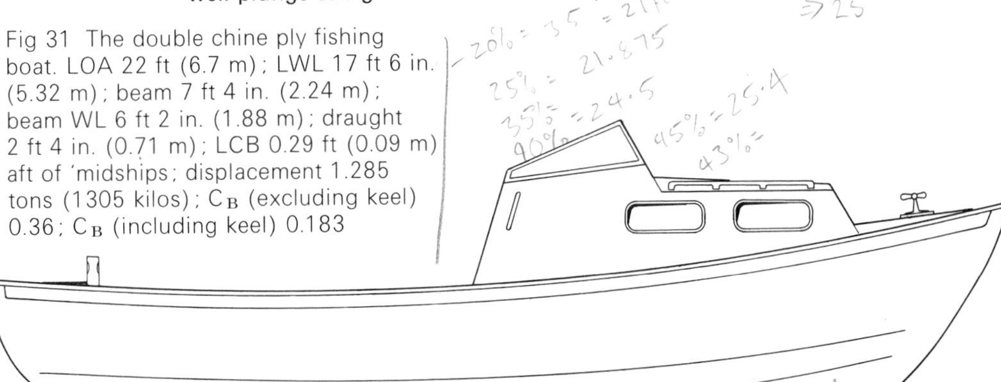

Fig 31 The double chine ply fishing boat. LOA 22 ft (6.7 m); LWL 17 ft 6 in. (5.32 m); beam 7 ft 4 in. (2.24 m); beam WL 6 ft 2 in. (1.88 m); draught 2 ft 4 in. (0.71 m); LCB 0.29 ft (0.09 m) aft of 'midships; displacement 1.285 tons (1305 kilos); C_B (excluding keel) 0.36; C_B (including keel) 0.183

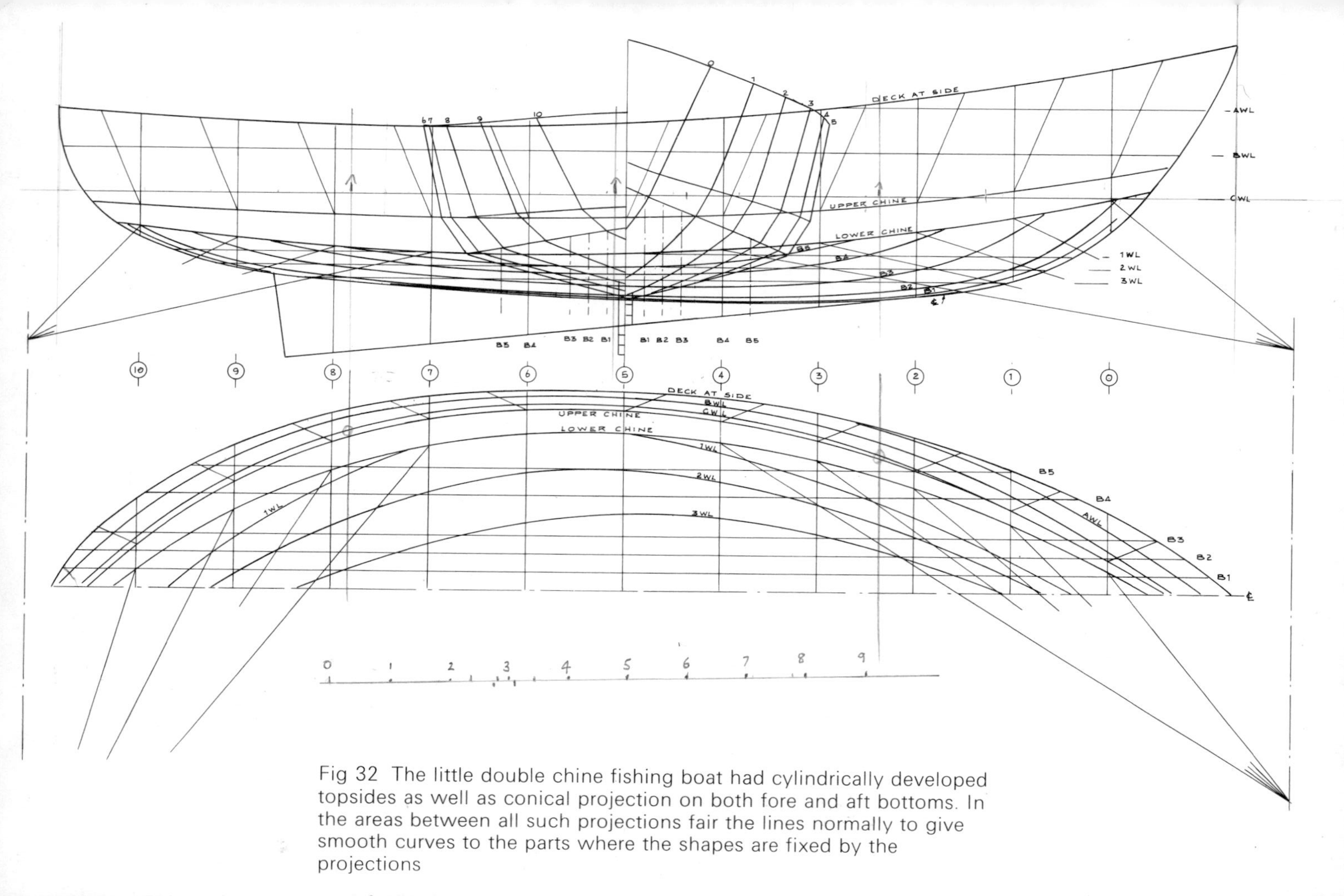

Fig 32 The little double chine fishing boat had cylindrically developed topsides as well as conical projection on both fore and aft bottoms. In the areas between all such projections fair the lines normally to give smooth curves to the parts where the shapes are fixed by the projections

A canoe-type performance can be achieved by powered craft, though they are always hampered by the weight of engines. For instance, the long, lean launches built by Camper and Nicholson between the Wars achieved very commendable speeds with remarkably little power. A 50-footer with 8 ft beam could manage 20 knots with 100 hp because it was lightly built and even this performance could be bettered today with modern motors though no one, to my knowledge, has attempted it. The growing trend is to make hefty and heavy hulls, fill them with all the comforts of home plus a few more and then put a couple of fuel-thirsty and expensive engines in the bilges to make up for all design deficiencies. Anyway, back to the fishing boat.

Speed Prediction for Non-Planing Craft

Table 7 can be used for working out speed knowing length, displacement and hull form. For example, take a boat 20 ft on the waterline and displacing 1.5 tons. If you look down under the column for canoe sterns it would appear that 5.7 hp would give 6 knots; that figure being the maximum theoretically possible with this form. These are calm water figures of course and an allowance must be made for emergencies and rough weather when at least 50 per cent more power may be needed to achieve a desired speed.

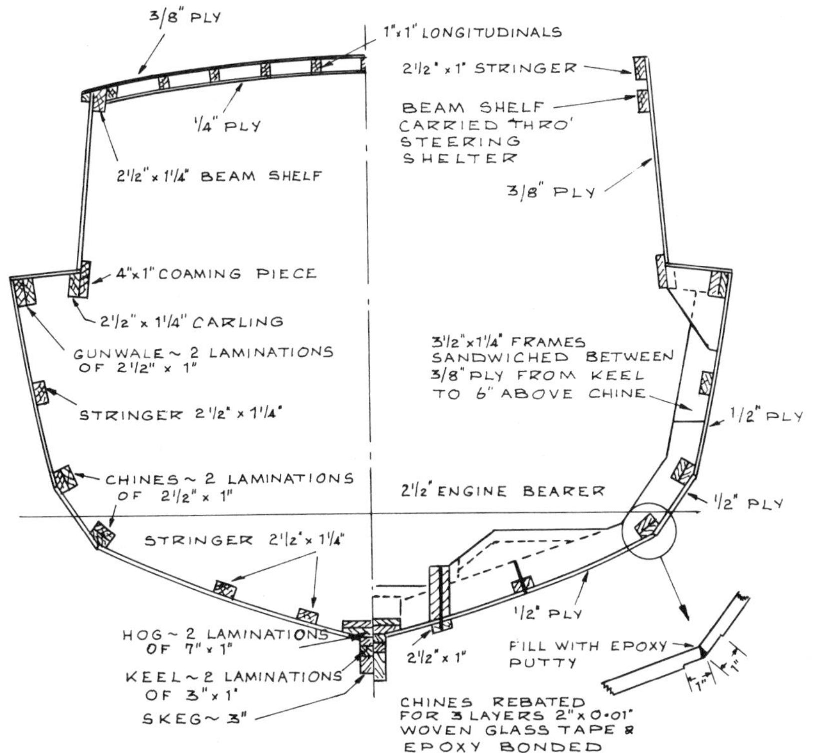

Fig 35 Structural 'midship section of the fishing boat

The table reproduced comes from the first edition of K. C. Barnaby's Basic Naval Architecture. For speeds higher than the range shown use either of the formulae given under Speed Prediction in the previous chapter.

Centre of Lateral Resistance

The lines plan of fig 32 is straightforward enough. The bottom forward and aft has been conically developed. The length between the areas where the projection has determined the shape is faired normally. The skeg or keel is brought well aft and this is important on vessels meant to be used offshore even though it does tend to increase the turning circle and to spoil precise astern-steering qualities. Without getting too technical it can be said that should the centre of lateral resistance (which is the centre of area of the underwater profile of the

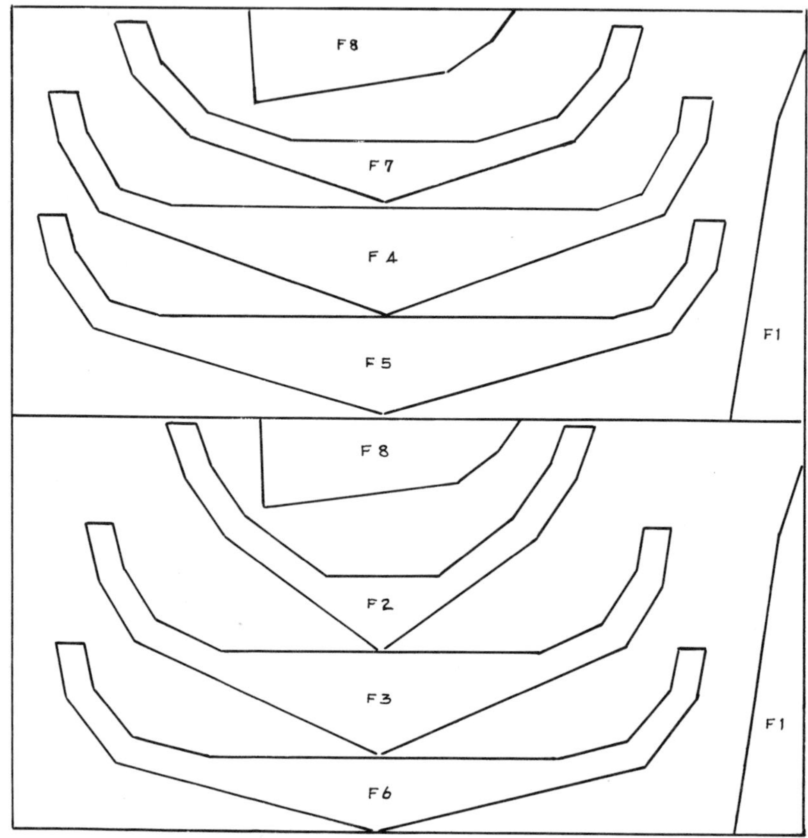

Fig 36 As reinforcing, and as an aid to accuracy, the frames were reinforced with ply. This is the way the reinforcements were cut from ply sheets

craft) be much ahead of the centre of gravity (LCG) when a yaw is started, as may happen when running with the seas, a turning moment is set up and unless controlled by a violent rudder movement the vessel will tend to swing round in a wide circle. This is typical broaching and can be dangerous in bad weather. So a raked skeg is required to bring the centre of lateral resistance (CLR) reasonably far aft and reduce the potential dangers which apply equally to sailing and power boats. Maybe the tendency of some modern fin and skeg yachts to broach repeatedly when running has this quite basic fact as one underlying cause.

Cylindrical Development

On the lines drawing of fig 32 there are straight lines drawn diagonally out from the intersection of chine and station lines in profile and plan. These are the basis of a cylindrical development whose object is to produce topsides that fall into the natural curves of a sheet material when bent between chine and sheer. The same objective as a conical development, in fact, but rather a quicker operation and especially applicable to topsides. Fig 33 shows how things are done.

Use the chine in plan and profile and the sheer in profile as the guide lines. What you are going to determine, then, is the deck line in plan and the curve, hopefully, of the rabbet at the stem. First draw lines out diagonally from the chine/station crossing points parallel to one another on the profile view and at, say, stations 5, 1 and 0. Next project the point where the diagonal crosses the deck line or sheer in profile vertically down to where it crosses the deck line in plan on station 5—or the station at 'midships if you had not used the 10-station system. From the chine/station crossing point in the plan view draw a diagonal to the deck line intersection and then more diagonals parallel to the first. Note that these diagonals in plan are not parallel to those in profile but each set must be parallel to one another. Then project down the profile intersections from stations 1 and 0 to the appropriate plan view generators and sit back and survey the result—which is normally diabolical at the first shot.

A freehand line or two and you will see which way things have to be altered to bring that plan view deckline somewhere near your requirements, so press on until you are satisfied and then fill in the missing lines at stations 0, 3 and 2. In some cases I have found that it is simply not possible to get the line you want right forward, for the deck line plan tends to be much wider than is desirable. When you have done the best you can, and that may take many shots, the correct shape between, say, station 0 and stem will simply have to be deformed to your desires.

Fig 33 also shows how to obtain the half-breadths of the waterlines from this cylindrical projection which will enable the sections to be drawn accurately and with the right amount of curve. On the boat under discussion the projection gave the shape shown, including the curve in the stem, but the constructional plan, fig 34, indicates a constructional method that can be employed if the projection does not please you forward, but to which you want to keep as far as possible.

False Stem. It will be seen that in place of a stem there is a bulkhead forward which lies at the same angle as the diagonal cylindrical projection line. The projection line selected would be the one nearest the bow which still accorded with the required curve of deck line. Forward again would be laminations shaped according to taste. Though this may seem to be carrying things a bit far, using a bulkhead does mean that the sometimes awkward bevelling at the stem is avoided and that the whole structure forward is immensely strong while ensuring that the sides sit happily along their planned lines.

Cylindrical development is important on steel construction where an

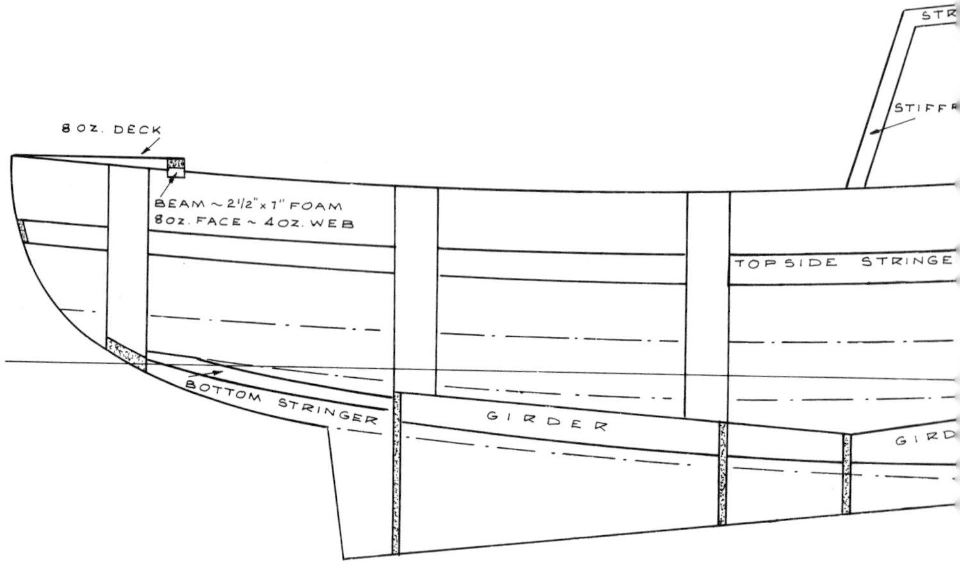

Fig 37 For a comparison to the way she was built in timber, here is a suggested G.R.P. construction. Though it is simpler, G.R.P. is not a cheap form of building and the boat would actually have cost a fraction more in glassfibre, even disregarding plug and mould costs

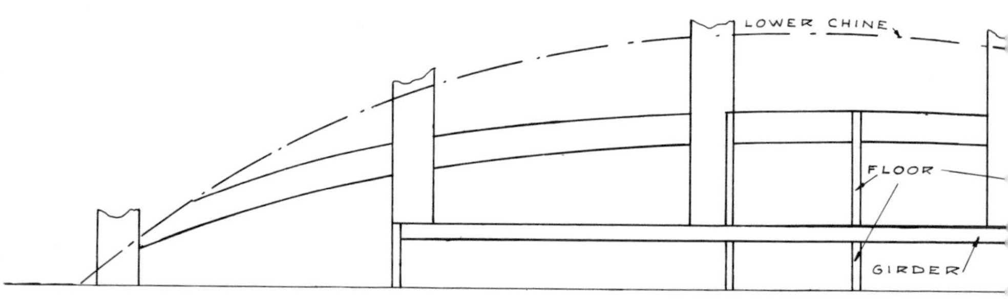

amateur builder may find it difficult to get the plates to lie down where he wants them and is reduced to making desperate temporary welds which finally serve only to distort the sheets.

Figs 35 and 36 show some more details of the construction of this little fishing boat while, purely as a matter of illustration fig 37 demonstrates G.R.P. construction for the same craft. There are a couple of interesting points raised by this drawing.

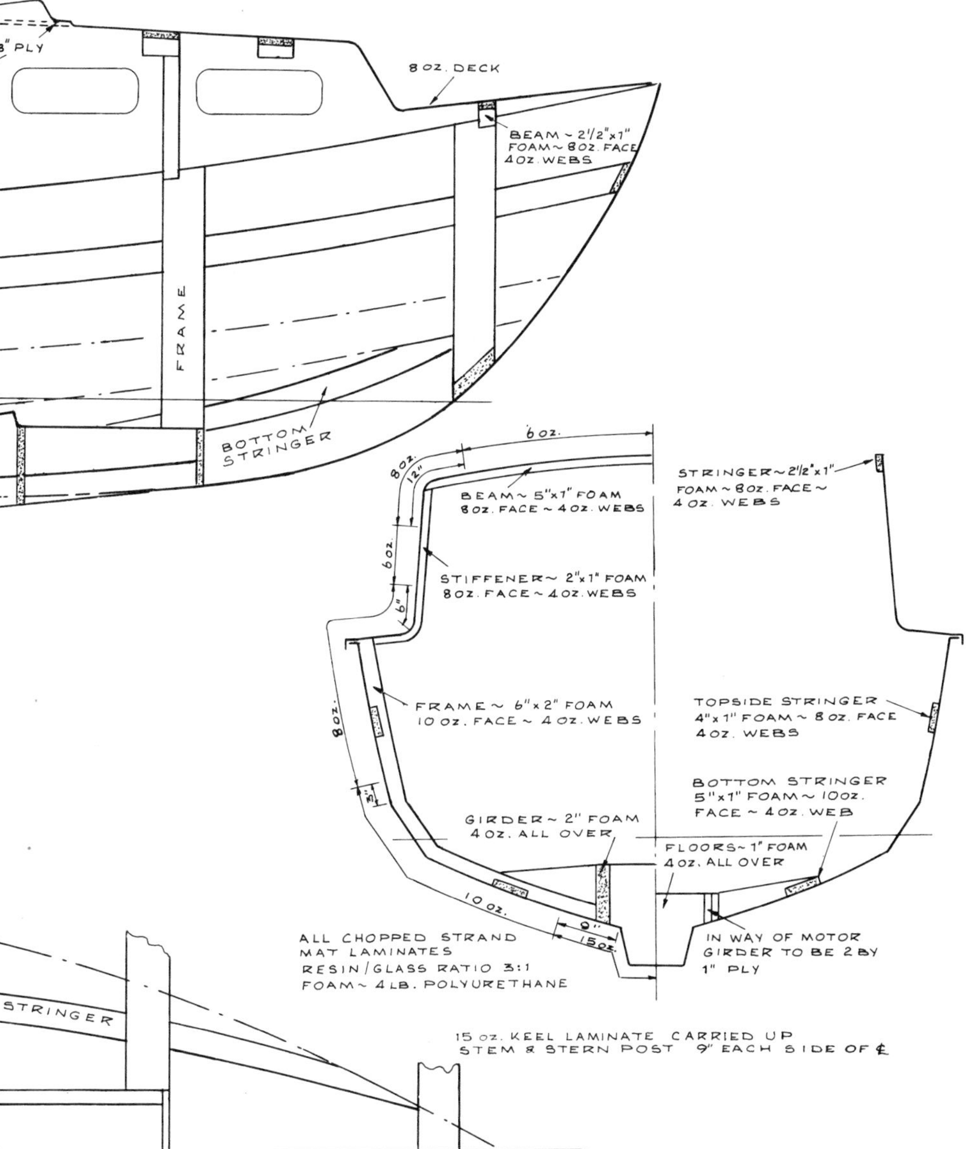

Ply versus GRP

The planking in the wooden version is $\frac{1}{2}$ in. (12 mm) thick and so weighs around 1.6 lb/sq. ft. Plywood has a modulus of elasticity, or E, of 1.8×10^6 lbf/in. Don't bother about what this means exactly, E is simply a measure of stiffness. If equivalent stiffness of another material is required its thickness is found by comparing their E's. E, the modulus of elasticity of a glassfibre laminate consisting of all-chopped strand mat as has been specified, is around 1×10^6 lbf/sq. in. If a mixed mat and rovings laminate had been used as in a more sophisticated construction, E would have been 1.4×10^6 lbf/sq. in.

Right, the method of comparison is:

$$\text{Thickness G.R.P.} = \text{thickness ply} \times \sqrt[3]{\frac{\text{modulus ply}}{\text{modulus G.R.P.}}}, \text{ therefore:}$$

$$\text{Thickness G.R.P.} = 12 \text{ mm} \times \sqrt[3]{\frac{1.8}{1.0}}, \text{ or } \sqrt[3]{\frac{1.8}{1.4}} \text{ in the case of mixed laminate.}$$

Thickness G.R.P. = 12 mm × 1.27 for all-mat,
or 12 mm × 1.087 for the mixed laminate.

That means for equivalent stiffness an all-mat laminate would have to be around 15 mm ($\frac{5}{8}$ in.) thick, or just a bit over 12 mm ($\frac{1}{2}$ in.) for the mixed laminate. Previously it was said that one ounce of laminate was $\frac{1}{32}$ in. thick, so for equivalent stiffness we would need 20 oz. of an all-mat laminate or about 17 oz. of the mixed laminate. If we took 3:1 and 2.5:1 resin/glass ratios respectively we would get the horrifying result that for equivalent stiffness to 12 mm ply weighing 1.6 lb/sq. ft, a mat laminate would weigh $20 + 60 = 80$ oz. = 5 lb/sq. ft.

while for a mixed laminate weight would be:
$17 + 42 = 59$ oz. = 3.7 lb/sq. ft.

This would make the G.R.P. boat far too heavy and we have to compromise with our consciences by calling the bottom lay-up just half that theoretically required weight at 10 oz./sq. ft. Obviously the hull will be much less stiff, but was the ply really too strong for the job? We shall see, but on all practical craft, especially work boats like this one, there must be a fair allowance made for wear and tear on the bottom.

Timber Scantlings

Lloyds Rules would agree that $\frac{1}{2}$ in. ply was correct. Table 8 gives a guide to typical timber scantlings based on the displacement of the craft in cubic feet. If we looked at the planking of the fishing boat again, recommended thickness is shown as $0.12 \sqrt[3]{D}$ for ply. Displacement in cubic feet is $1.28 \times 35 = 45$ cu. ft.

$$\text{Thickness} = 0.12 \times \sqrt[3]{45} = 0.12 \times 3.56 = 0.43 \text{ in.}$$

That is a bit under $\frac{1}{2}$ in. but is near enough for all practical purposes. The only conclusion we can draw from all this is that even at 10 oz./sq. ft the G.R.P. boat is going to weigh more than the ply version, for in broad terms about one-third can be added to planking weight in both cases to allow for framing. Fig 24 back in Chapter 2 showed a recommended thickness of around 9 oz./sq. ft for this size of power boat so we should be safe.

Chines and Floors

Before we leave this boat it might be sensible to have a quick look at the various chine and floor arrangements that are possible. Chines are obvious enough—being the lengths of timber that provide a jointing surface at the chine angles—but floors are actually structural members that tie the two halves of the boat together across the keel. Fig 38 refers.

With ply planking especially, it is important to prevent water getting at the raw edges and this is the reason for the glass tape and epoxy resin shown in the first sketch and also used in the fishing boat just described. Epoxies are much better stickers-to-wood than polyester resins, hence the suggestion. Sometimes one sees a combination of steamed or laminated timbers and hard chine form especially on high speed motor boats and that is where the last two figures in the chine row would be likely to occur.

Floors are normally used on every timber or frame and are one of the most important parts of the structure, though frequently overlooked or shoved in, undersize, as an apparent afterthought. They are equally important in G.R.P. construction and can be seen on fig 37 spanning the hollow skeg and clamping the two halves of the boat together. The bottom two rows of fig 38 give various methods and constructions but

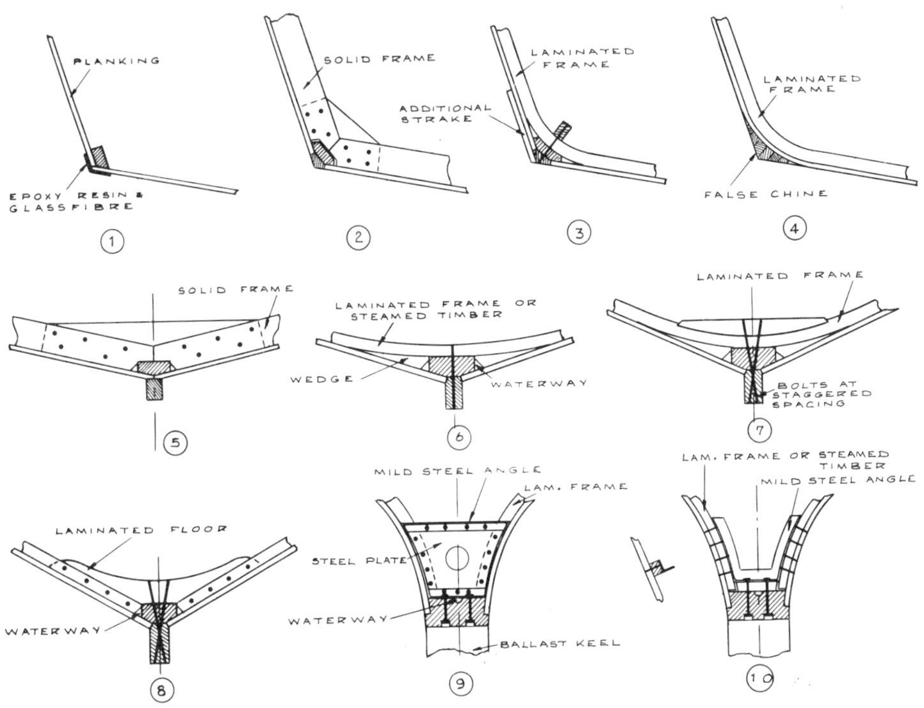

Fig 38 Typical chine and floor structural schemes for timber-built vessels

as (6) and (7) show, if the frame can be carried across the keel the floor piece itself can be quite simple. On lightly stressed craft it is usually enough merely to put wedges under the timber or frame as in (6). Of course, this scheme of continuous frames can only be managed towards the stern of very flat-floored vessels and even there if a mizzen is set or backstays stress the hull in the area or a big engine is installed it is sensible to reinforce the frame as in (7).

Enough of these technicalities. It would be a relief to look at a picture once again and for the first and only time in this book to discuss an accommodation.

29 ft (8.8 mm) STEEL KETCH

We once built a swim-ended cruiser for sheltered waters' use and the plans were published. A boat builder on the Grand Union Canal saw the drawings and asked me if I could give him some help in translating the requirements from the original ply construction into steel. This was done and he proceeded to build a couple of cruisers which performed to both our satisfactions but not, it seemed, to that of potential customers who were interested but not keen to part with their money for something that was not conventional. It is extraordinarily difficult to sell a boat that does not accord with what buyers are used to seeing, however overwhelming may be the advantages of the new look.

Anyway, that is by the way. The boats were eventually sold. Some time later the builder approached me again. He said that there were 50 firms building steel canal cruisers and while he still had plenty of customers for his standard range he would like to try something entirely different which would let him diversify into a new market if things became too competitive for comfort. After a bit of discussion we decided on a motor sailer, dimensions being governed mainly by the size of his slip, and figs 39 to 45 illustrate what emerged.

At the time of writing there is no end to the story for the builder found that demand for his canal boats did not slacken and though he constructed the hull quickly, and well, he never had enough time to finish it. No doubt if someone had come along waving a large cheque he would have done something about it but customers for this type of boat do not, as a rule, expect to find anything in canal-side premises and it would have taken quite a bit of money and effort to promote the craft in the right quarters. So it remained unfinished until a man bought the hull as it stood to finish off at home. He is making a good job of it, incidentally.

(*Opposite*)
Fig. 39 The wishbone ketch. Steel tripod and hollow wooden masts are of roughly equal stiffness. LOA 29 ft (8.83 m); LWL 23 ft 4 in. (7.1 m); beam 9 ft 3 in. (2.82 m); beam WL 8 ft 2 in. (2.48 m); draught 4 ft (1.22 m); LCB 0.835 ft (0.025 m) aft of 'midships; displacement 5.23 tons (5300 kilos); C_B (excluding keel) 0.4; C_B (including keel) 0.24; sail area 390 sq. ft (35.6 sq. m); sail area/displacement ratio 130

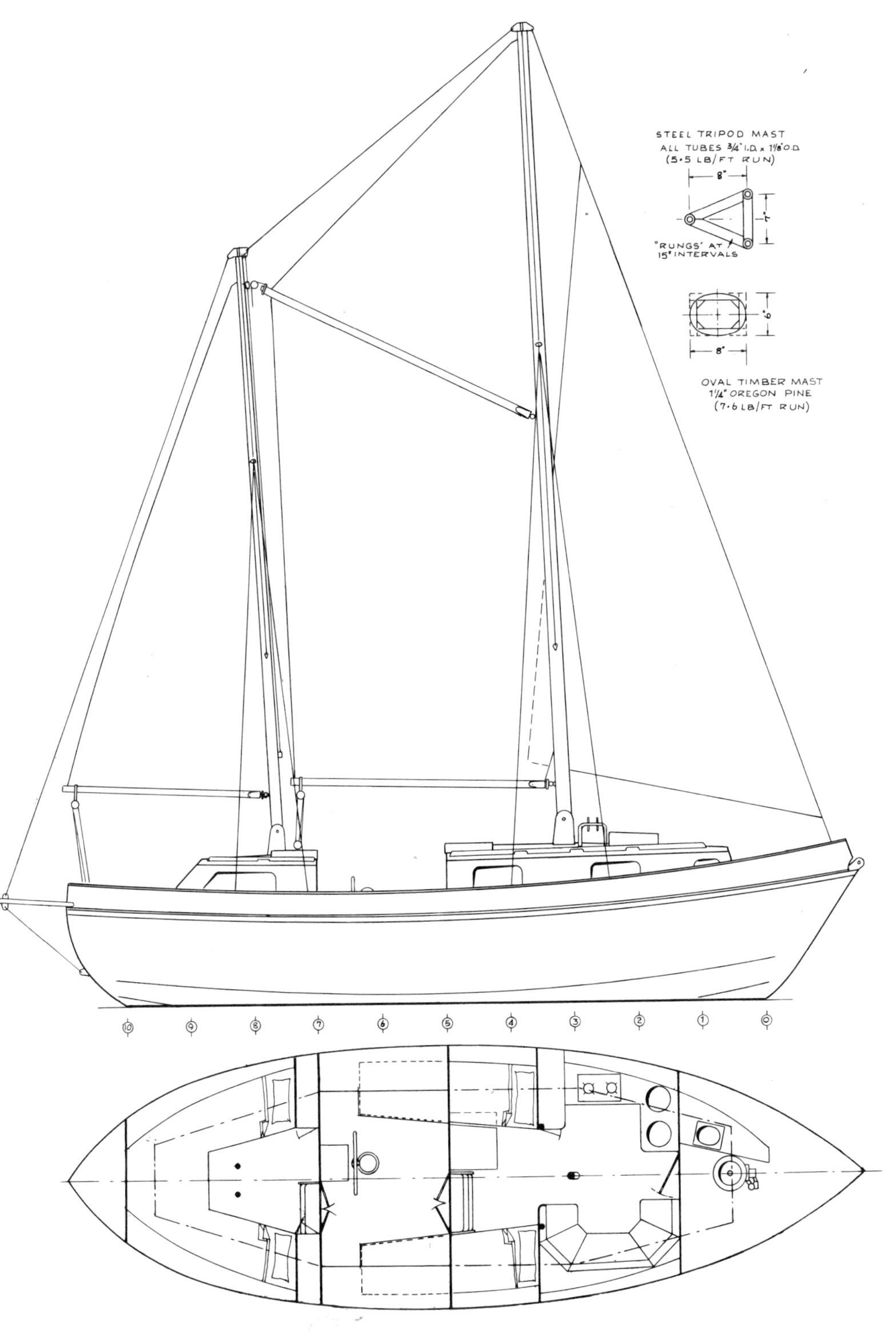
STEEL TRIPOD MAST
ALL TUBES 3/4" I.D. x 1 1/8" O.D.
(5·5 LB/FT RUN)
8"
7"
"RUNGS" AT 15" INTERVALS
6"
8"
OVAL TIMBER MAST
1 1/4" OREGON PINE
(7·6 LB/FT RUN)
10
9
8
7
6
5
4
3
2
1
0

I wish I could have put more outright success stories in this book but those are generally associated with G.R.P. craft designed for easy production and not with 'one-offs', especially those with a construction or some other feature of particular interest to the amateur designer. This motor sailer demonstrates simple, modern steel building and so we had better get on with it.

Looking at the profile, accommodation plan and the lines of figs 39 and 40 it will be apparent that it has practically nothing in common with

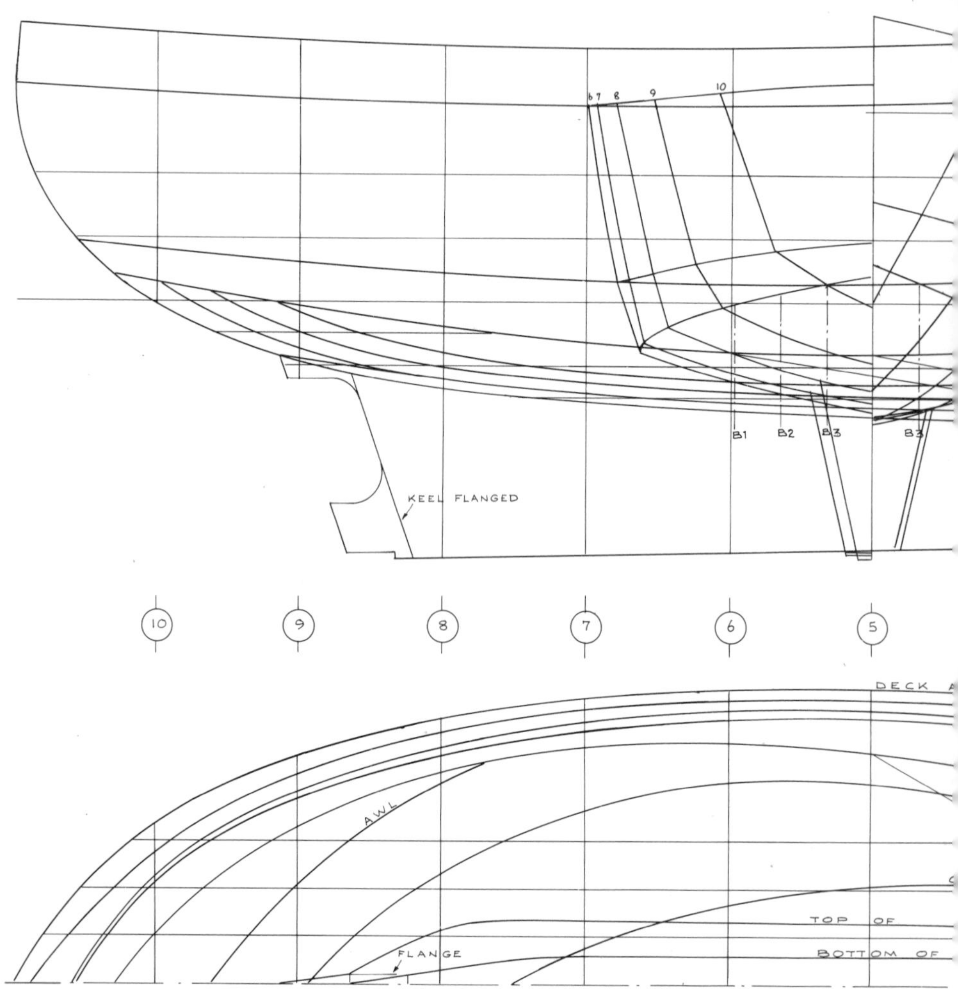

Fig 40 Lines plan of the double chine steel ketch. Though the topsides were cylindrically developed the generator lines are not shown

the production boats that are usually shown in the yachting journals. These craft are very often influenced by the rating rules and the designer, urged on by the sales manager, will be drawing something that can, at a pinch, be used for racing with at least an outside chance of success. He will also be told that on a craft of this size at least six berths are needed with the possibility of a seventh. Consequently there will be a dormitory-style layout while the hull shape will be arranged to achieve low girth measurements at the strategic points; to have as

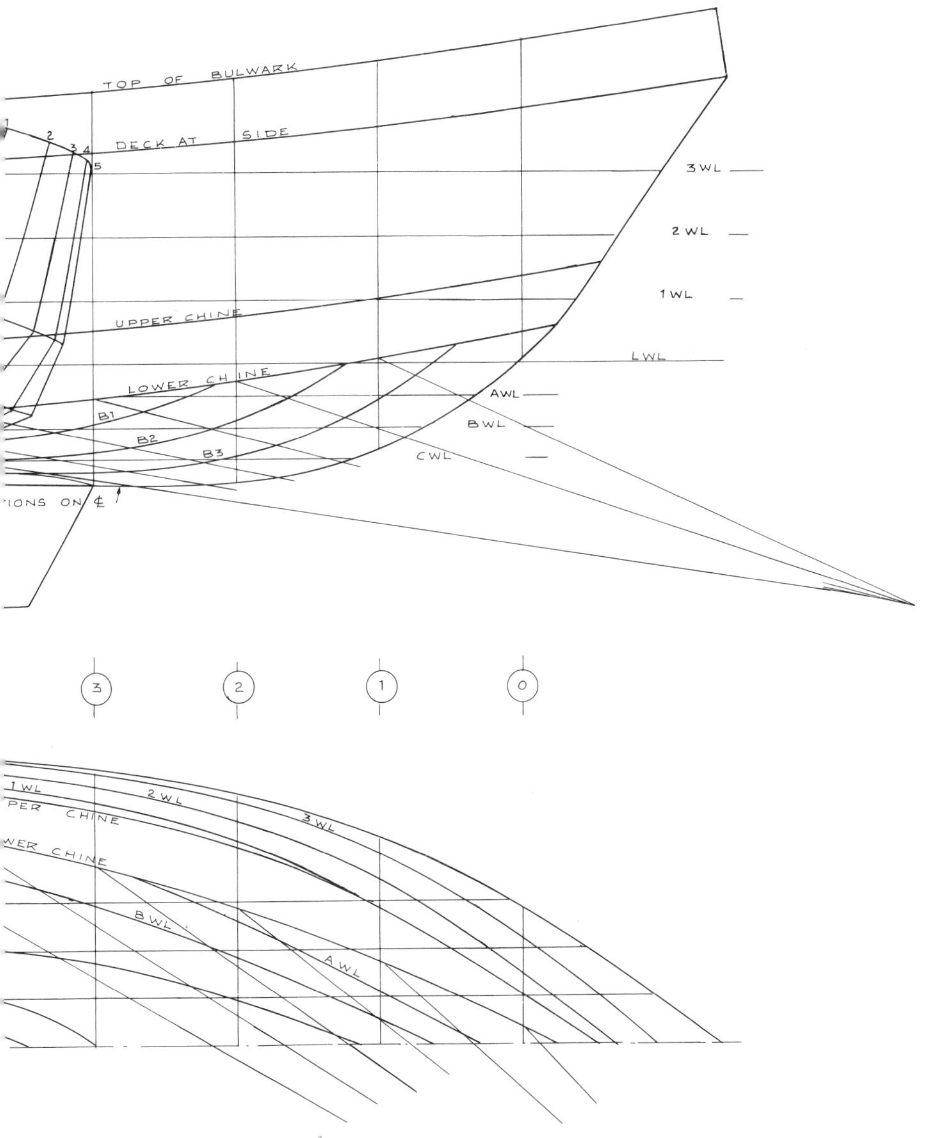

little wetted surface as possible; and to be adequately stable but no more. An arc of a circle gives the smallest amount of wetted surface for a given displacement which is why the sections of many modern racing boats look as if they have been drawn with a pair of compasses. Such a shape achieves its various objectives but is not ideal for a cruising vessel as it restricts space inside and does nothing to dampen rolling. As you can imagine, a barrel would be the ideal roller and a modern yacht designed with the IOR rules in mind is often little more than a sophisticated barrel with a fin keel attached.

Sail Area/ Displacement Ratio on Cruising Yachts

The average fast cruising yacht has a sail/displacement ratio ranging from 160 to 175 on waterline lengths from 20 to 40 ft. This is $\frac{SA}{D^{\frac{2}{3}}}$ where SA is actual sail area in sq. ft and D is displacement in tons. Full working sail would be counted here, and if a small genoa was normally carried, for instance, that would be included. The motor sailer here has a sail area of 390 sq. ft and a displacement of 5.23 tons so its ratio is $390/5.23^{\frac{2}{3}} = 130$. In Chapter 4 there is a 40 ft ketch illustrated which has a much more conventional yacht appearance than this one so we can postpone discussion on the finer points of sailing design until then, but the comparatively low sail area ratio brings this steel ketch into the motor sailer category.

Rig. A type of wishbone ketch rig is used, the main being in one piece despite it looking like a topsail above a gaff main, and sets up inside a wishbone gaff. The outer end of the gaff is attached via a block to a jackstay which runs up the forward face of the mizzen mast. With this, the gaff can be trimmed so that it sets roughly parallel to the boom and does not sag off to leeward. The main can be reefed in the normal way until the wishbone is down to the boom gooseneck, at which point it is time to take the whole thing off anyway. The jib is set on a boom and is self-tacking for it seems to me that for the motor sailer concept the rig should be easy to handle and not require strenuous work on winches. The masts have been kept reasonably short and though they could, of course, be alloy extrusions they could equally well be of timber or of a triangular section of steel pipe welded together. Both are illustrated on fig 39.

The decks are bounded by bulwarks which are simple to arrange on steel construction and give people on board a sense of security while disguising the height of the cabin sides. Bulwarks also provide an excellent base for mounting stanchions or guard rails.

Accommodation. The layout below allows me to illustrate the few prejudices I have left over the matter of accommodation. All the others have gone as things I thought right or read as being the most suitable have been shown to be only one arrangement of many possible variations each one of which finds favour with different but equally experienced owners. On this 29-footer there are only four berths but there is a decent spot for lounging opposite the galley. Bunks cannot be the right height and width for both sleeping and sitting comfortably, and though they normally have to perform this dual function if it can be avoided the vessel will be more genuinely habitable for long periods. The galley itself should be set out so that the cook can brace himself in varying directions. The one shown would have a rail running fore and aft in way of the stove so that the operator can be wedged against rolling. Two sinks are shown for if you put things down on a draining board they promptly fall off at sea.

There are pillars (black circles on the plan) through the accommodation which act as stiffeners for the cabin top and as grab rails. They should be arranged so that one can lurch from one to the other without having to let go entirely. Though not shown on the sketch ventilation is important and for this boat there would need to be at least one ventilator in the toilet space forward, two in the saloon plus one over the galley and a further two in the aft cabin. Three-inch mushroom vents would be about right. They can be screwed shut in bad weather. The toilet space forward may cause some raised eyebrows because the motion at sea will be most felt right up in the bow but one gets used to that after a while and the advantage of having proper elbow and leg room seems to me to outweigh the disadvantages. In any case boats spend far more of their time in harbour than they do slogging it out offshore in really bad weather. Incidentally, the box shape on the aft, port main cabin bulkhead is a chart table with a hinged section over the bunk. It is simple enough to arrange a stool like a shooting stick that drops into holes in appropriate spots both under the table (where it is out of the way) and in front of it when chart work is required.

Variable Pitch Propeller. This boat has a 22 hp diesel specified with a feathering and variable pitch propeller. According to table 7 that should be capable of driving the boat at its maximum hull speed with stacks in reserve. The variable pitch propeller is quite useful on a motor sailer where pitch can be adjusted to suit the speed of the boat to give the best results without, perhaps, having to run the motor at very low revolutions when it may set up unpleasant vibrations. The idea of being able to feather a propeller is that the blades can be set fore and aft so that they offer the least resistance to the water when sailing. On most motor sailers a shaft lock is sensible to stop the propeller revolving when under sail alone. Unless the shaft can turn really quite fast, implying very free-running and accurately aligned stern gear, there is usually less resistance with a fixed propeller. In addition if a hydraulic gearbox is installed it does it no good to have a driven shaft without the engine running and supplying oil pressure.

Propeller Diameters

Fig 40 shows the lines plan. It is all pretty obvious but one query comes to mind immediately. How big an aperture has to be left in the skeg for the propeller, or to simplify that question still further, what propeller diameter is needed? In some cases an engine manufacturer's pamphlet describing his product will suggest suitable diameters but otherwise table 9 may help.

Let us say that this 22 hp motor develops its power at 2250 rpm and that the gearbox has a built-in 2:1 reduction. The propeller is thus turning at 1125 rpm. Look down the left-hand column of table 9 until 1125 rpm is reached. Actually this will have to be taken as between 1000 and 1200 rpm. Now look across until a figure somewhere 22 hp emerges. Well, there is 23 hp at 1200 rpm and 24 hp at 1000 rpm with propeller diameters of 16 in. and 18 in. respectively. Thus, we could guess at 17 in. diameter and be near enough. Without going into lengthy explanations about propeller design the subject of pitch is best avoided but any propeller manufacturer will make a recommendation if given whatever details he considers necessary.

Shaft Diameters

It might be handy to know shaft diameter, too, for then the stern tube can be selected from a catalogue and this, in turn, will give the size of the flange at its aft end which will determine how wide the aft end of the skeg must be. Obviously it must be wide enough to house the flange, but no more. A rough idea of prop. shaft diameter can be gained by dividing the propeller diameter by 13. Thus, on this boat we had a 17 in. propeller and so the shaft would be $\frac{17}{13}$ or 1.3 in. Shafts normally go up in $\frac{1}{8}$ in. increments so we would need one approximately $1\frac{1}{4}$ in. diameter. In these metric days you can convert that 17 in. prop. to 430 mm. Shaft diameter would then be $\frac{430}{13}$ or 38 mm. A word of warning, though; a variable pitch arrangement was specified for this boat and on these the control shaft usually runs through the centre of propeller shaft whose diameter may consequently be increased. Check on that if the need arises. Recommended shaft sizes apply to bronze and stainless steel types. Propeller blade clearance from the bottom of the hull or skeg should be about 15 per cent of prop. diameter.

Steel Construction

Still on this 29 ft ketch, the construction plans of fig 41 to 45 apply. Steel is a very stiff material whose modulus of elasticity, E, is 30×10^6, compared with that of 1.0 or 1.4×10^6 for G.R.P., 1.8×10^6 for ply (all as already mentioned in the section Ply versus G.R.P.) and 10.5×10^6 lb/sq. in. for aluminium alloy. Consequently it needs very little framing on craft below, say 40 ft (12 m) in length even when using the steel in thin sheets. The difficulty has traditionally been that it was difficult to get the proper shape of the craft without frames, and framing in conjunction with a thin steel shell showed through in the classic 'starved dog' manner.

However, things have progressed and with a bit of effort steel boats can be made virtually without any framing at all as on the motor sailer.

First of all it is necessary to make a full-sized half-model, fig 41. The

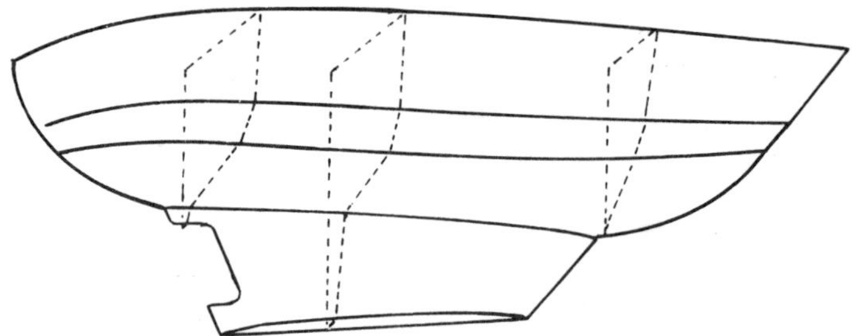

Fig 41 Before building a steel craft of frameless construction a full-sized half-model in timber and hardboard is made

moulds, probably taken as being on the stations to save any additional measurements, are made and fastened to a base board. They are notched in the usual manner to take chines, gunwales and longitudinals at the top and bottom edges of the skeg. These are put in to ensure fair curves everywhere. The half-hull is subsequently carefully sheeted in hardboard; these sheets forming patterns for the plating. If the hardboard templates were correct the subsequent steel sheets must fit on the actual boat and they can be cut direct from the templates.

Temporary frames (welded pipe is probably easiest) are then erected upside down on a base. These frames are not attached to the hull but serve mostly to give something to lean the plating against while it is being positioned. If the boat is not so large that it is impossible to handle full-length sheets they are best welded into one length now and, say, the bottom panel laid over the frames each side. Next either the skeg side or the panel between the chines is held in the appropriate place and chocked up if necessary. Very short, temporary welds are made along the jointing edges, bending as you go, until the whole thing is joined. Repeat the process with all other panels but do no continuous welding until everything is together. If things get too difficult spot welds to the frames might be necessary but do these unwillingly and only as a last resort. Finally continuous welds may be made along all the butts with a backing weld on the inside. There are no permanent frames at this stage but the hull will be quite stiff enough to turn right way up. Now knock out the pipe frames and replace with framing, bulkhead boundaries and whatever else is felt desirable, using intermittent welds. There have been no chine bars, stem bars or anything else, nor will there be.

The same frameless construction is used for cabins and decks. Pin rails, handrails, hatch coamings and pillars provide all the stiffness needed.

Priming. Remember to put a pillar under the mast if it is stepped on deck. This boat had 3 mm steel throughout, except the bottom of the skeg where it was 6 mm so as to resist possible abrasion. The boat was built outside to allow nature to do the work of the shot-blaster in removing mill scale. A coat of epoxy paint primer on all bare surfaces after the mill scale had gone and after wire brushing provides the basis for all subsequent paintwork.

A heavy coat of bitumastic paint on the skeg interior allows concrete to be poured in without future problems of corrosion.

Weight Proportions. On this vessel steel plating, including decks, cabin sides and tops, floors and brackets, weighed 2918 lb.

Steel framing such as bulkhead boundaries, stringers, pillars and hatch coamings weighed 640 lb. That is about 22 per cent of the plate weight and is a considerable reduction on normal methods where framing commonly comes to 33 per cent of the shell weight, whether in timber, G.R.P. or framed steel.

The woodwork here, which included bulkheads, cabin soles and odds and ends amounted to 660 lb. The bulkheads were 12 mm ply, incidentally, and the soles 1 in. softwood.

Joinery totalled 730 lb but included such things as the galley stove and sink and linings in exposed positions.

The grand total of weights including the engine, 25 gal. of water and 50 gal. of diesel fuel and various things not mentioned here such as tanks and spars was 7522 lb or 3.36 tons.

Keel Centre of Gravity and Weight

Leading on from the weights table came the problem of weight and positioning of the concrete ballast. Table 10 shows the final stages of the weight calculation and then the method of finding out where the centre of gravity of the ballast should lie. In this it is aided, I hope, by the little sketch of fig 42. This shows how the weights were distributed on the motor sailer and since the weight and distances acting upwards must be balanced by those acting downwards we could say:

Ballast weight × L + Total weight ex. ballast × M = Displacement × N

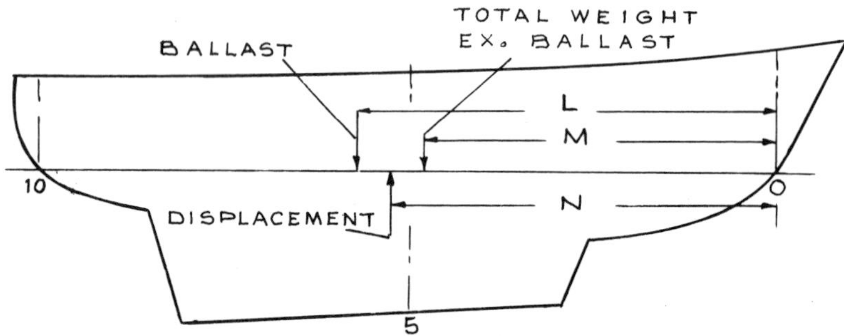

Fig 42 Sketch showing the dimensions used when working out the correct position for the longitudinal centre of gravity of a ballast keel

Back to table 10. Moments (and if you have forgotten what those are, they are the distance the centre of gravity of a piece of equipment or a part of the structure is from a given point multiplied by the weight of the piece of equipment or part of the structure), were taken from station 5. Hence there were some moments forward and some aft. The rest of the calculation follows fairly obviously.

We found that the centre of gravity, or centre of area, of the concrete ballast must lie 14.2 ft aft of station 0 and it must weigh 1.87 tons, which is 4200 lb. If concrete weighs 150 lb/cu. ft then we need 4200/150 = 28 cu. ft of concrete, supposing there were no scrap additions. Normally the builder would cut up scrap steel and chuck it in with the concrete to increase its density. Provided he does this evenly throughout all will be well. The hollow skeg is fairly symmetrical so there is no problem in finding the centre of area of the ballast, but the next chapter shows how it is done on a metal keel.

So much for that. Now we might have a brief look at rudders since they feature on figs 45 and 46.

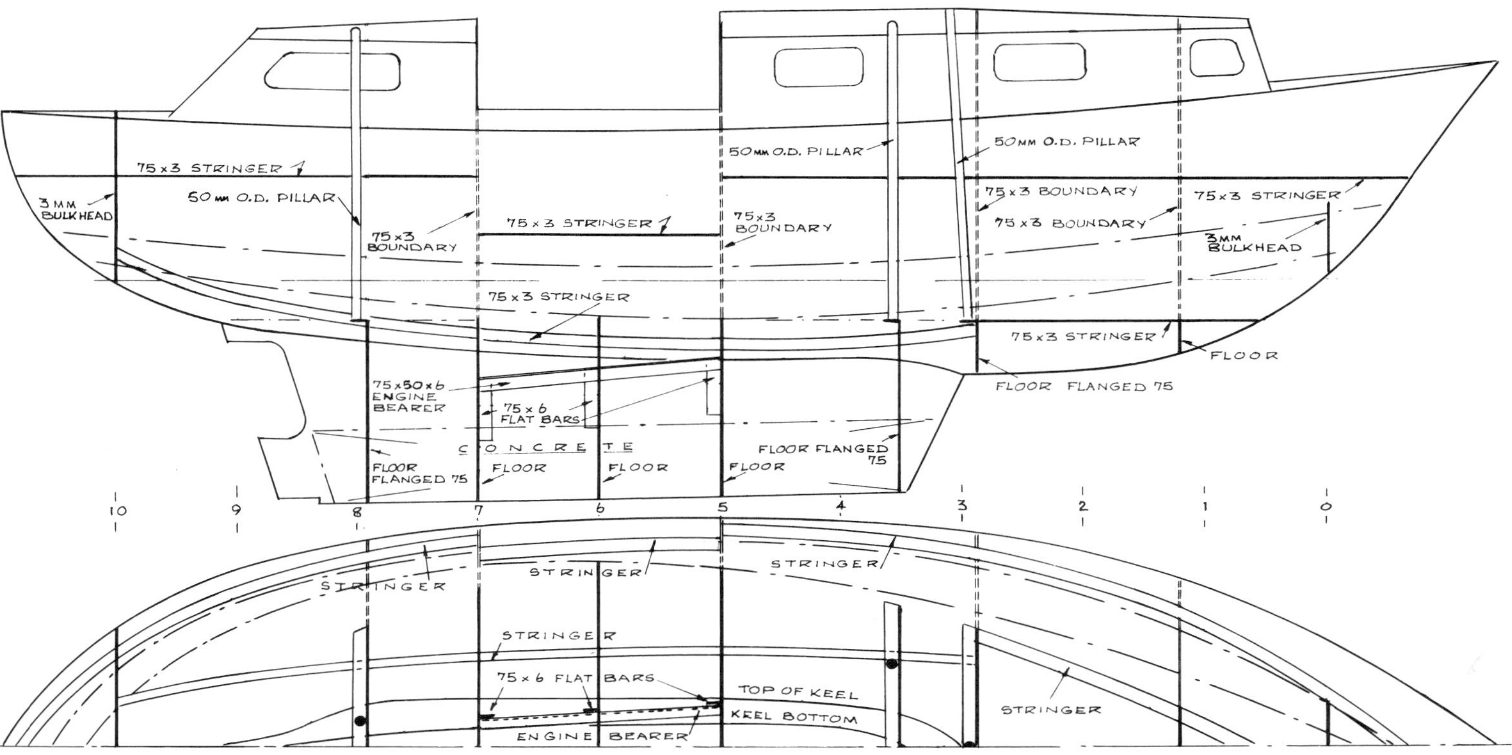

Fig 43 Outline construction plan of the ketch. Dimensions are in millimetres

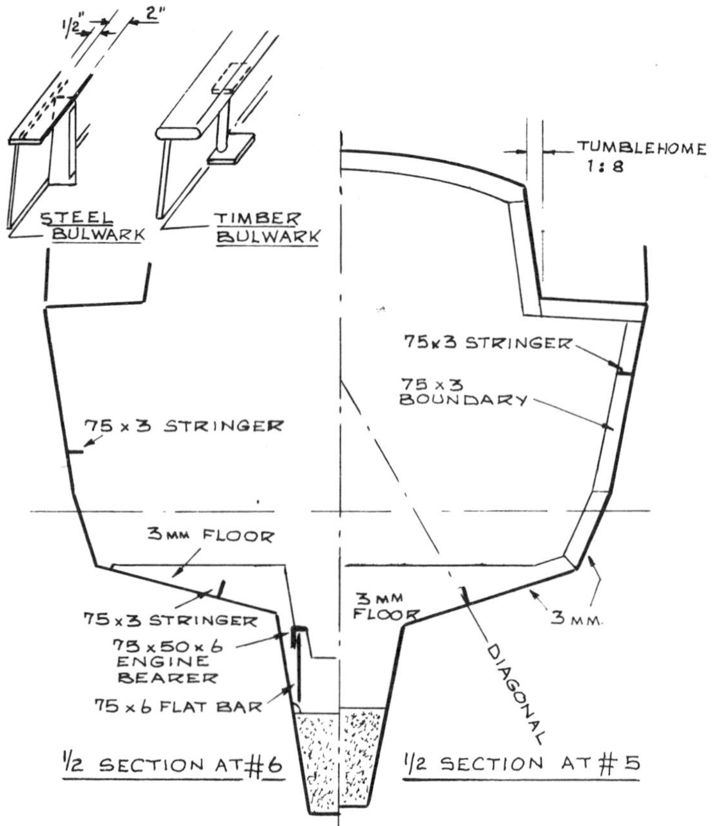

Fig 44 More constructional details on the steel ketch. Ply bulkheads are bolted to the boundaries. Steel bulkheads would be too heavy and present problems in their decorative finishing though at the aft peak where the area involved is small it is easier and cheaper to use a steel bulkhead. This shows on fig 43. The two little sketches show method of attaching bulwarks to decks. On the left a steel deck can have a flanged plate welded to it but if the deck is wood sheathed the bulwark support will probably have to have a base

Rudders, Stocks and Steering Gear

Before considering any other feature, a few suggestions for sailing boat rudder area might be in order. Generally speaking, dinghies and other small centreboarders need comparatively big rudders of the order:

$$\frac{\text{Rudder Area}}{\text{Area of Lateral Plane}} = \frac{1}{7}$$

The area of lateral plane is simply the profile area of the underwater body of the boat—the shaded area of fig 47. So, if the lateral plane area was 15 sq. ft, rudder area should be $\frac{15}{7} =$ a little over 2 sq. ft.

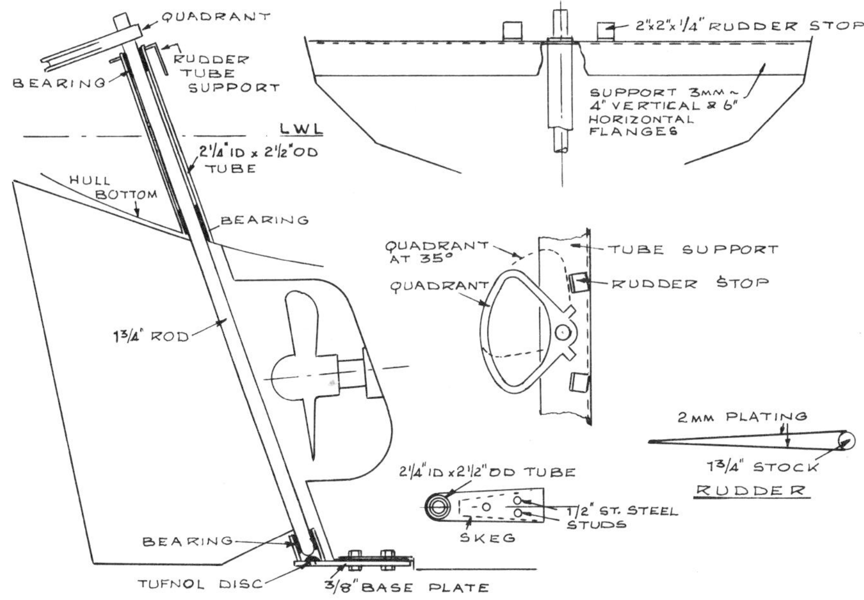

Fig 45 General details of the aft end of the ketch and some idea of the rudder and quadrant arrangement

On cruising boats where the rudder is normally hung behind a skeg or on a fin, the ratio can be changed to:

$$\frac{\text{Rudder Area}}{\text{Area of Lateral Plane}} = \frac{1}{10}$$

In that case an underwater profile area of 50 sq. ft would lead to a rudder area of $\frac{50}{10} = 5$ sq. ft.

On power boats the situation is a bit more complicated since the area of rudder must bear some relationship to speed. The faster the boat the smaller the rudder in fact. For low speed motor boats like the one in this chapter an approximation would be to use the same area as for a sailing vessel. However, there is a formula which is quite useful for speed/length ratios of up to about 3. Above this figure it is a bit erratic but is still usable with discretion. If it looks right, it probably is, on very fast craft. Anyway, if you can face yet another formula, here it is:

$$\text{Area} = K\sqrt{\frac{D}{0.01 \times L^3} \times \frac{\sqrt{L}}{100V}}$$

where K is a constant varying from 2 at 20 ft length to 18 at 100 ft length; V is speed in knots; D is displacement in pounds; and L is waterline length in feet.

We could try out the sum for the little fishing boat in this chapter where waterline length was 17.5 ft; displacement was 1.28 tons

(2870 lb); speed we could say is 6 knots; and K we can take as 2. Then:

$$\text{Area} = 2\sqrt{\frac{2870}{0.01 \times 17.5^3} \times \frac{\sqrt{17.5}}{100 \times 6}} = 2\sqrt{\frac{2870}{53.5} \times \frac{4.18}{600}}$$

$$= 2\sqrt{0.373} = 2 \times 0.612$$

Therefore rudder area is 1.22 sq. ft.

If you will now cast your eyes towards figs 45 and 46 a few more details are shown. First of all, it is rarely sensible to draw fancy, curved shapes. The bottom trailing edge of a rudder does more work than any other part of the blade so that might as well be kept square (as opposed to being rounded off) while definite straight line boundaries to the rudder will enable it to play its proper part in increasing lateral resistance.

A rudder can be astonishingly thick and still be efficient so that in

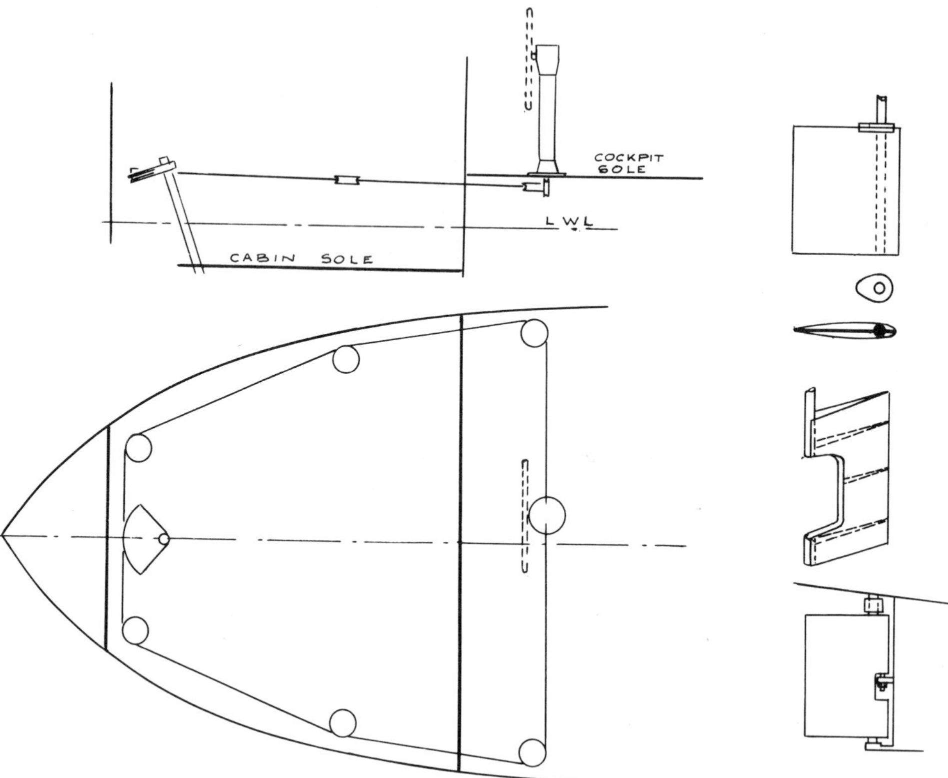

Fig 46 Chain and cable steering was used on the ketch. The right-hand sketches show rudder schemes which are further explained in the text. The rudder one above the bottom is an example of how easily a steel rudder can be fabricated to accommodate a cut-out for a propeller

nearly all cases the stock can be carried down at its full diameter to the bottom with advantage.

Fig 45 shows that the blade on the motor sailer was simply steel plates welded to the stock at the leading edge and to each other at the trailing edge. The top sketch of fig 46 shows the scheme of welding either arms or a continuous thin plate to the stock and then covering everything with timber to achieve a fair curve. This one is a balanced rudder with some area (which should not exceed 20 per cent of the total) ahead of the stock. A balanced rudder is not quite as efficient as an unbalanced affair like the one below it on fig 46 and needs about 10 per cent more area to make up for its deficiencies but it is easier on the helmsman, for once the rudder has been twisted slightly the area ahead of the stock will assist in the turning process.

Unshipping the Rudder. Fig 46 at the top shows a spade rudder in that it has no bottom bearing. This affects the stock diameter as will be seen in a moment, but the point here is that it must be possible to remove a rudder if required without chopping the boat to pieces or digging a trench in the mud below. With a spade rudder, and other types as well, a jointing flange can be made at the top of the rudder so that the rudder and the top half of its stock can be separated at this point. The two halves of the flange are bolted together. The bottom sketch shows another way of achieving the same objective on a rudder complete with gudgeons, pintles and bottom bearing. It must be possible to lift the rudder out of its bottom bearing and that means that there must be clearance at the gudgeons, pintles and between the top of the blade and the hull. But since we certainly don't want this lifting to happen accidentally the clearance gap between the top of the rudder and hull bottom must be partially filled with a loose sleeve. The sleeve is in two halves, perhaps held together by big hose clips.

Fig 45 showed a different way of allowing a rudder to be unshipped. Here the plate holding the bottom bearing is set into a recess in the skeg and can be freed by undoing three studs. The rudder stock comes down with the rudder in this arrangement which may not always be satisfactory. It would be fine on a slip, for the exposed stock is not very long, but could raise problems if the boat was sitting on the mud.

Materials. Various bearings are shown on fig 45 and these could be of Tufnol, Ferrobestos or nylon. If the top of the tube housing the stock is not a fair way above the waterline, a stuffing box will have to be introduced at its top. Such things are available commercially and can be found in many chandlers' catalogues. As for materials for the stock and tube, I must confess that I favour mild steel. Cheap, cheerful, easily machined and welded and amenable to flame-sprayed deposits of other metals if required. Thus, the stock could have a layer of stainless steel sprayed on at the bearings and at the point where it cuts the waterline and is most liable to rust. Alternatively two or three coats of epoxy paint would do quite well there, especially if you have arranged it such that the rudder can be dropped easily for inspection. Of course the stock could be galvanised and though this may make fitting through bearings a little difficult the bearings in this area can be quite a sloppy fit without disadvantage. The stock tube also can be mild steel swilled out with epoxy paint before fitting the bearings.

Rudder Stops. Figs 45 and 46 also show the steering gear of the motor sailer, which is a chain and cable set-up with the cable running through big sheaves. This is the cheapest arrangement and completely satisfactory as long as it is ensured that all the wires run smoothly and the sheaves are properly lined up and bolted into position. With cable steering a quadrant is usual at the rudder stock though a tiller could be employed. In any case there must be stops to prevent the quadrant or tiller turning more than about 35 degrees either side. Not only does a rudder become steadily more ineffective above that angle but the whole gear may be damaged if the rudder can swing hard over. It could do that in, say, the process of broaching and just when every ounce of control is needed. So make sure the stops are strong and properly secured.

Stock Diameter. So far we have skated round the diameter of rudder stock needed, but taking a deep breath we had better have a look at this now and prepare to do yet another bit of mathematics. Yacht designing may well be more an art than a science, and long may it remain so, but it seems impossible to escape the rigours of calculations for very long. Fortunately, though the work involved looks pretty tedious when set out in a book, it only comes along at intervals when actually designing, leaving one breathing spaces to regroup the faculties.

The things we need to know about a rudder before getting down to the sums are its area A in square feet; the distance of the centre of area of the rudder aft of the centre line of the rudder stock or the axis about which it turns in feet; the speed of the boat in knots multiplied by 1.2, this figure being V; and the distance of the centre of area below the lowest bearing in the hull when dealing with spade rudders. These are rudders without a bottom bearing and the distance we want is in feet.

Pressure on rudder, $P = \dfrac{1.8 \times A \times V^2}{2240}$ tons

Twisting moment, $T = P \times$ centre of area aft of axis (ft) $\times 12$ (inch tons)

Bending moment (spade rudders only), $B = P \times$ centre of area below bearing (ft) $\times 12$ (inch tons)

For twisting moments only (that is on rudders with a bottom bearing):

$$T = \frac{1}{16} \times \pi f \times d^3$$

where f is allowable stress in rudder stock material. For mild steel $f = 8$. Turning that sum round so that we get d, the rudder stock diameter, on its own and recalling that π is $\frac{22}{7}$:

$$d^3 = \frac{T}{\frac{1}{16} \times \frac{22}{7} \times f} = \frac{T \times 16 \times 7}{22f} = \frac{112T}{22f}$$

and so $d = \sqrt[3]{\dfrac{112T}{22f}}$ or $\sqrt[3]{\dfrac{56T}{11f}}$

That gives a rudder stock diameter in inches.

If a spade rudder has been used we have to combine the bending and twisting moments, to give an equivalent twisting moment:

Combined bending and twisting, $T = B + \sqrt{B^2 + T^2}$
and again:

$$d = \sqrt[3]{\frac{56T}{11f}}$$

An example might clear the fog. Let us assume a rudder of 3 sq. ft, A = 3; on a boat travelling at 10 knots so 1.2 × 10 = 12 = V; the centre of area is 6 in. (0.5 ft) aft of the axis. It has a bottom bearing so:

$$P = \frac{1.8 \times 3 \times 12^2}{2240} = 0.347 \text{ tons}$$

Twisting moment, T = 0.347 × 0.5 × 12 = 2.18 inch tons.

To find the required mild steel rudder stock:

$$d = \sqrt[3]{\frac{56 \times 2.18}{11 \times 8}} = \sqrt[3]{1.39} = 1.117 \text{ in. say } 1\tfrac{1}{8} \text{ in.}$$

If this rudder had no bottom bearing we would have to consider the bending moment, B as well; and suppose the centre of area of the rudder was 1 ft below the bottom hull bearing:

B = 0.347 × 1 × 12 = 4.16 inch tons.

Using that figure and the previous twisting moment to find the equivalent twisting moment:

$$T = 4.16 + \sqrt{4.16^2 + 2.18^2} = 4.16 + \sqrt{22.15} = 4.16 + 4.71$$
$$= 8.87 \text{ inch tons}$$

Again we want to find the rudder stock diameter, d:

$$d = \sqrt[3]{\frac{56 \times 8.87}{11 \times 8}} = \sqrt[3]{\frac{495}{88}} = 5.63 = 1.78 \text{ in.}$$

Breathing a sigh of relief that that is over, the calculation for the size of pintles is much more simple. These pintles might occur on a transom-hung rudder or midway up an inboard rudder as in fig 46. The calculation is the same in either case and the pintles must, of course, be associated with adequately strong and matched gudgeons. The pintle is the bit with the pin in it.

$$\text{Sectional area of pintles in sq. in.} = \frac{\text{weight of boat (lb)} \times 0.4}{1000}$$

So, if the boat had a displacement of 2 tons, the pintles would be:

$$\frac{4480 \times 0.4}{1000} = 1.8 \text{ sq. in.}$$

The area of a circle is $\frac{\pi d^2}{4}$ where d is the diameter and π is $\frac{22}{7}$. So if we know the area we can find the diameter:

$$\text{Diameter} = \sqrt{\frac{\text{area} \times 7 \times 4}{22}} = \sqrt{\frac{\text{area} \times 28}{22}} = \sqrt{\frac{\text{area} \times 14}{11}}$$

We know the area was 1.8 sq. in. so:

$$\text{Diameter} = \sqrt{\frac{1.8 \times 14}{11}} = 1.51 \text{ in.}$$

Spars

There has been quite enough calculation so far with a little more to follow so I don't intend to go into formulae for determining mast and rigging sizes. In any case these days when most spars are of aluminium alloy their manufacturers will give anyone buying from them an indication of a suitable rigging plan and will, of course, supply adequately strong spars as a result of their own calculations. They will want the sail plan and the displacement tonnage plus a deck plan to work out the best places for rigging attachments.

The tubular steel tripod mast shown on fig 39 is quite strong enough for that boat and can be simply adapted up and down the scale for bigger or smaller craft. The three legs of the mast are joined at, say 15 in. intervals by pipe, tying the legs together and forming climbing rungs. Such masts are normally stepped on deck and the legs converge towards the base, coming nearly to a point, and are set into a fabricated steel base plate. Though not the last word in styling or efficiency a tripod mast goes quite well with the sturdy, steel cruising boat type.

Diameters and Rake. A section through a hollow timber mast is also shown on that figure. A rough guide to such things is that the wall thickness should be about one-fifth the mast diameter, or mean diameter if it is oval. The outside diameter would be around 0.02 of overall length and the mast should be parallel-sided for about one-third the distance between deck and where the main jib halyards connect. From there it can taper to something like three-quarters of its greatest diameter at the masthead. If a track is used the taper must be on the forward side of the mast. All this assumes adequate rigging and a glance at similar craft to the one you are designing will give plenty of clues as to how to arrange this. For short, unstayed solid masts, the diameter ought to be increased to something like 0.03 times the overall length.

All masts must rake for the sake of appearance and a mizzen must rake more than the main if the illusion is not to be that the two are leaning in towards one another. A suitable rake to begin with is 1 : 35 for single-masted rigs and, say 1 : 25 for ketches, yawls and schooners.

Boom diameters might be about 0.015 times their length and if roller reefing is to be used they should, ideally, be thicker at the aft end than forward. Suitable taper might be 0.8 times diameter at the sheet block attachment and 0.7 at the gooseneck. The maximum diameter ought to occur halfway between the sheet attachment and the gooseneck, for that is where the bending moment will be greatest. A gaff has something like the same proportions but is normally parallel-sided. Should you want to go in for this split gaff scheme of the motor sailer—in fact a wishbone—the distance between its arms would be around 18 per cent of its length, but it would be advisable to consult the sailmaker on its precise shape. There is quite a lot to be said for making a wishbone of thinnish-wall steel tube wrapped in P.V.C. tape to avoid possible rust marks, with the end fittings of welded steel fabrications.

Centres of Effort and Lateral Resistance

Finally in this chapter we can try and ascertain where the centres of lateral resistance (CLR) and effort (CE) are and where they should lie in relation to each other. Fig 47 is the one to look at now.

The centre of lateral resistance is really the centre of area of the underwater profile—the part with diagonal lines on fig 47. To find this point cut the outline from a piece of tracing paper, fold it lengthways a few times to stiffen it, and then balance it on a needle or the point of a compass leg or something. Prick the point through the paper and that is the centre of area. It helps if you draw in station 5 or whichever station is at 'midships before folding and balancing. This point is assumed to be the spot around which the hull pivots under sail.

Now for the centre of effort. There are various ways of finding this point but as we have spent a lot of time working out moments (distance times area or weight) we might as well continue that way.

First the area of each sail and its individual centre of area must be detected. Triangular sails are easy but if you have an odd-shaped sail like the main on Fig 47 divide it into triangles. Ignore the roach and

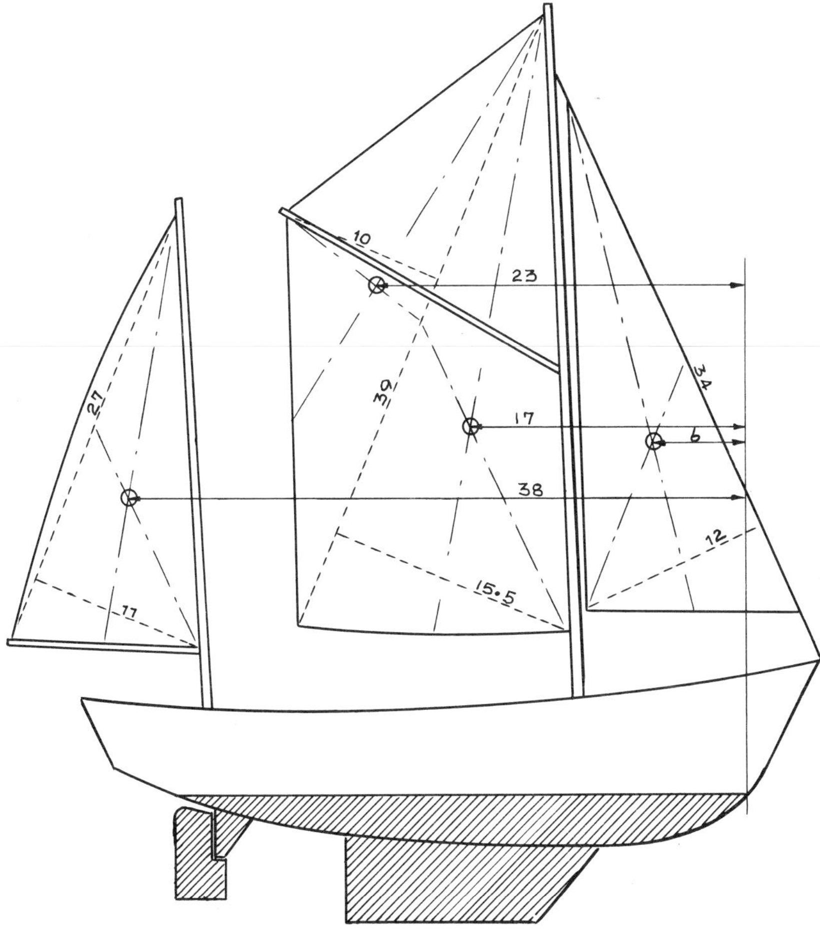

Fig 47 The shaded part is the lateral plane area and it is cut out and balanced on a compass point to find the centre of lateral resistance (CLR)

assume all sails have straight-line edges. The area of a triangle is the length of its base multiplied by half the perpendicular height. If we look at the jib, its luff, which we can call the base is 34 ft (or even 34 m) long and a vertical from it to the opposite corner is 12 ft or metres long. Hence the area of the jib is:

$$34 \times \frac{12}{2} = 204 \text{ sq. ft or sq. m.}$$

From now on we will call everything feet but exactly the same mathematics will apply if dimensions are taken in metres. The main has been divided into two triangles with a common base of 39 ft. One vertical measures 10 and the other 15.5 ft. So the area of one triangle is:

$39 \times \frac{10}{2} = 195$ sq. ft and of the other $39 \times \frac{15.5}{2} = 303$ sq. ft.

The mizzen follows the same pattern:

$$27 \times \frac{11}{2} = 149 \text{ sq. ft}$$

To find the centre of area of a triangle divide two of its sides in half; draw lines from the opposite corners to these spots; and the crossing points of the lines give the centre of area. This has been done on each sail or part of a sail on fig 47.

Now erect a vertical through, say, station 0 and draw in horizontal lines from the centres of areas to the vertical and measure the distances. Again those measurements are shown on fig 47. Multiply each distance by the area concerned (take moments in other words), add the totals and divide the whole lot by the total sail area. This will give you the distance in feet the combined centre of effort lies from station 0. This would be the sum from fig 47 and the areas already obtained.

$$\frac{6 \times 204 + 17 \times 303 + 23 \times 195 + 38 \times 149}{204 + 303 + 195 + 149} = \frac{16522}{847} = \frac{19.55 \text{ ft aft}}{\text{station } 0}$$

Please don't try to work out a scale for fig 47, as it is not drawn to one, but let us assume that the waterline length was 38 ft and that the centre of lateral resistance (CLR), which we found by balancing, lay 5 ft aft of station 5 ('midships). If the waterline length is 38 ft then 'midships is 19 ft from station 0 and the combined centre of effort (CE) falls 0.55 ft aft of it. Thus the 'lead' of CE over CLR is $5 - 0.55 = 4.45$ ft. Expressed as a percentage of waterline length that is $\frac{4.45}{38} \times 100 = 11.7$

'Lead'

The recommended 'lead' varies from about 10 per cent (0.10 times waterline length) for shallow hull, fin keel or centreboard yachts, and probably the motor sailer just fits into that category; to about 6 per cent for cruising yachts of normal form. In fact many modern ocean racers which are basically shallow hull, fin keel types have 'leads' of up to 15 per cent and so one cannot draw a line and say 'Stop there'. The figures given can be used as a general guide, though, and it would be unwise to depart from them radically. The 40 ft ketch of the next chapter might also qualify as a shallow hull craft and it is only a really heavy displacement yacht that would need as little lead as 6 per cent.

4. Round Bilges

On slow and medium-speed vessels a well-designed round bilge form is the most efficient in that its resistance in pounds per ton of displacement should be lower than on its chine rivals. This applies up to a speed/length ratio about 2.5 or 3.0 though the boat is likely to roll more easily and through a greater arc than hard-cornered types. Above such a speed it pays to have flat surfaces and abrupt changes in shape for these, as has been mentioned, deflect spray and check water running up the sides, both of which add to wetted surface and increase resistance. Interestingly, too, on very fast power boats it has been found that even a slight rounding of the keel in section can lead to high-speed rolling which is unnerving to say the least.

Water clearly prefers to travel round curves rather than knuckles and shoulders and so virtually all top-class sailing yachts, which spend much of their lives travelling at speed/length ratios below 1.0, are round-bilged. It is no more difficult to draw the lines of such a vessel than those of a chine boat though it will certainly take longer for there are a great many more curves that will need accurately fairing. As with all lines plans it is probably best to draw the 'midship section first and then two more stations, one towards the bow and the other somewhere near the stern. On a 10-section plan that means that stations 1, 5 and 8 are sketched in as a trial run and a couple of waterlines and buttocks quickly drawn in to see how things are turning out. If all is well, add two more sections to correspond with those waterlines and buttocks and then, no major alterations appearing to be needed, put in a few more waterlines and another buttock. In this way the boat is drawn mainly on its fore and aft lines with the sections only used to check their fairness. Do remember that the crossing points of buttocks and waterlines must agree in plan and profile and try and get a realistically-wide rabbet line.

Ignoring Rabbet Width. Here I had better make a confession. All along I have been burbling on about rabbet lines, their width and so on and so forth. What was said was the correct way to do things but, if you have been looking closely at some on the lines plans reproduced, you might have noticed that the sections sometimes come to a point on the sectional centreline, with the waterlines also coming to a point on the plan view centreline. This is the lazy way out. You draw the lines as if the structure does not exist and only afterwards put in the various widths. The result is a boat perhaps slightly shorter and shallower than intended, though the difference will be quite small of course. This is, I understand, wholly reprehensible but it does the job if you are careful. In the case of a steel vessel without stem or keel bar, the plating to all intents and purposes will come to a point. With G.R.P. construction the stem will normally end on a radius—as it did with the rigid-bottom inflatable—and the keel will either come to a shallow vee or have a definite radius. It is only on timber-built craft that this rabbet line business really matters and then you can either do it properly or fudge the job.

Still, I am delighted to see that the first example in this chapter was drawn in text-book fashion.

23 ft FISHING LAUNCH

For some reason I seem to get quite a few designs for fishing boats and this is one of them. Quite unlike the canoe-stern double-chine job of Chapter 3 this craft, fig 48, has what is called a semi-displacement hull. That is, it is suitable for speeds well above the governing speed/length ratio of 1.34 but not as high as planing velocities. Back in table 7 a speed/power/displacement relationship was shown and the right-hand column was headed 'Transom and Very Flat Stern or Chine Form'. Well, a semi-displacement hull comes into that category. A round bilge boat planes indifferently and is wasteful of power for various reasons but mainly because of that excess wetted surface business mentioned a little earlier. Looking again at table 7 and taking this craft as 20 ft on the waterline with a displacement of 1.23 tons, it would appear that maximum speed will be about 14–15 knots and that around 50 hp will be needed to achieve that. As this boat is outboard driven, and that was the intention from the start using as a maximum 25 hp, I don't know what sort of speed she is really capable of but if one was seriously aiming for that 15-knot figure it might be sensible to harden the turn of the bilge towards the stern and particularly at the transom so as to produce something more like a hard chine form. Anyway, in the shape shown she has pleased her owner and won quite a few converts among the fishing fraternity of her local port who had previously been accustomed to more traditional types, either double ended or with very narrow transoms and aft waterlines coming to a point. An inboard engine could be fitted, of course.

(*Opposite*)
Fig 48 Fishing boat with semi-displacement hull form. LOA 23 ft 1 in. (7.05 m); LWL 20 ft (6.09 m); beam 7 ft 4 in. (2.24 m); beam WL 6 ft (1.83 m); draught 1 ft 3 in. (0.383 m); LCB 0.1 ft (0.03 m) aft of 'midships; displacement 1.23 tons (1250 kilos); C_B 0.45

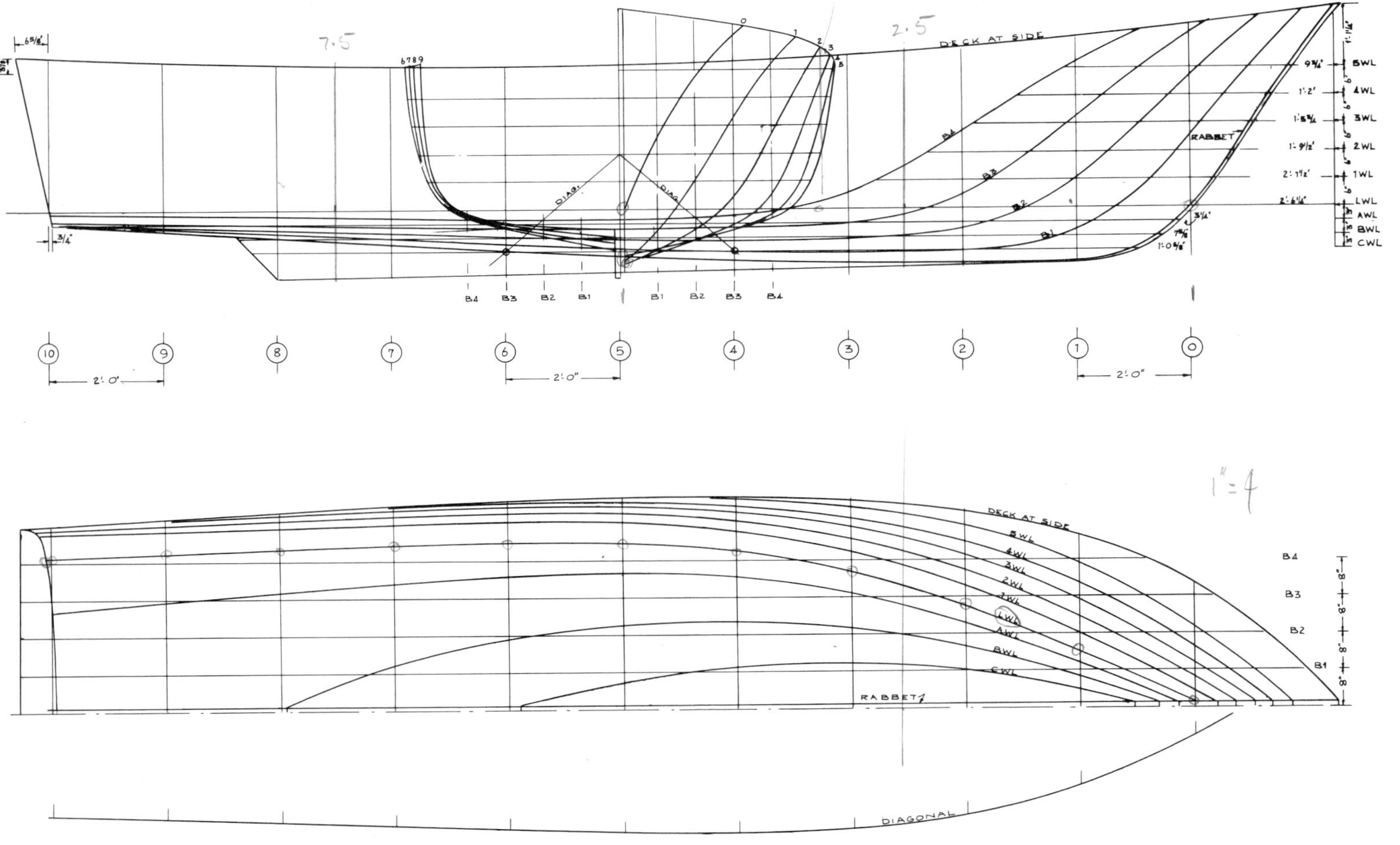
DECK AT SIDE
RABBET
5WL
4WL
3WL
2WL
1WL
LWL
AWL
BWL
CWL
DIAG.
B1
B2
B3
B4
0
1
2
3
4
5
6
7
8
9
10
2'-0"
RABBET
DIAGONAL

Balancing the Ends

The flaring topsides promote dryness and the forward waterlines are quite full. The point here is that though a leaner entrance would create less resistance any boat that has a wide stern and is meant to go to sea in most weathers must have a fair amount of buoyancy forward to balance the enormous amount aft. The consequences of failing to match the two ends are that in a following sea the wide stern will be easily lifted and unless the bow buoyancy can in some way resist this lift, the stem will be shoved way down in the water with a consequent rapid forward shift in the centre of lateral resistance. This will, as has been indicated, convert an initial yaw into a full-scale broach. Though a motor boat has been shown here to illustrate the point that was only because the full waterline aft shape is exaggerated in a semi-displacement hull and gives a good example. Precisely the same action takes place in a sailing vessel with the full stern lines common today. A lean bow may well be less resistful and allow the high speed required of a racing machine but a following sea will create endless problems for the helmsman which are best avoided when designing a cruising yacht.

In a similar vein, fine bow lines and full stern waterlines tend to make for a wet boat when going to windward for the bow, needing to be lifted by the seas can't manage it because the stern won't be induced to sink. Consequently the seas will tend to come aboard. As with all yacht designing there have to be compromises all the way. The waterline aft must be quite full to resist squatting at speed/length ratios of 1.34 or over; to keep wave-making resistance down (this is a technical point rather beyond the scope of this book); and to cater for the fact that weight is commonly concentrated aft on a yacht. Forward waterlines should be fine for least resistance but not so fine as to reduce forward buoyancy a dangerous amount. There will be a little more on this subject when we get to a suitable example of a sailing cruiser at the end of this chapter.

Sheer Line

But now briefly back to the fishing boat. There is no separate above-water profile drawn as this was an open boat and practically everything can be seen on the lines plan. A brief word about sheer or deck lines . . . because a boat is coming to a point at the bow there is an optical illusion that causes the sweep up of the deck line forward to look less than that drawn on the lines plan. Consequently the upward curve should be slightly steeper at the forward quarter of the length than along the rest of the deck. If a straight line sheer is drawn, in practice it will look as if it is drooping at the bow. The same applies to the stern, of course; to a lesser degree if there is a transom but equally as much with a double-ender.

Trim Angles

Since any boat tends to settle itself in the water so that the buttocks are lying flat on the water, this craft, with flat buttock lines running roughly parallel to the waterline, would want to trim quite flat. This is right for sea-keeping in rough water but not so good in every case from the pure efficiency point of view. In fact, a fast boat ought to trim bows up at three or four degrees for least resistance and one of the reasons for transom flaps on offshore planing boats is to try and achieve the best trim for different conditions. Assuming that the vessel trims normally at, say, four degrees with the throttles open this will be the correct attitude for running downwind. With her bows up and stern down the CLR will be well back and handling ought to be easy. On the other hand at this angle she is travelling with a fair amount of exposed bottom forward and is liable to be thrown about by head seas when going to windward. Consequently the flaps are operated to force the bows down, when efficiency will fall and resistance will increase, but comfort will be greater. Since the hammering felt by the crew is enough to cause quite serious injuries at real speed in rough water anything that can reduce the pounding will be worth the drop in efficiency.

Cold Moulding

Fig 49 shows a structural 'midship section of this boat as well as a half-section of a typical building mould. Construction is cold-moulded with three skins of $\frac{3}{16}$ in. (4 mm) ply laid over a former and glued together. This makes for a tough and homogenous structure and one that is very suitable for an amateur builder, being quick and straight-forward. Lloyds allow a reduction in planking thickness of 10 per cent for cold moulding together with a 25 per cent reduction in frame

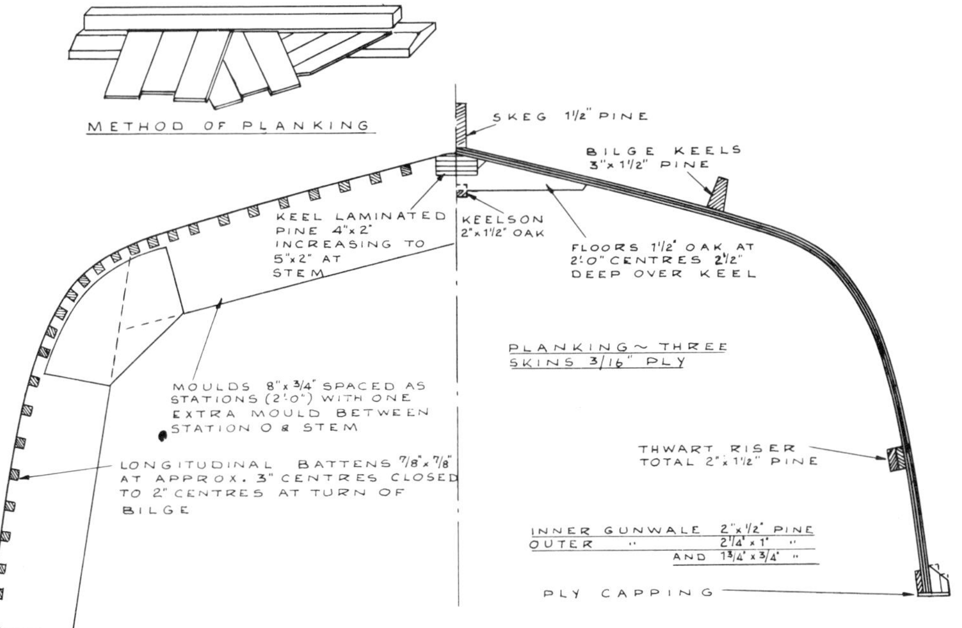

Fig 49 'midship section of the 23 ft fishing boat showing on the left-hand side the construction of the building mould. Three skins of ply were employed but veneers would be a good alternative. Any number of skins, over three, may be used in cold moulding and sometimes the outermost layer runs fore and aft for the sake of appearance.

strength or, alternatively, if the normal framing is carried out, planking thickness may be reduced by 25 per cent. In any case frames are required and these are rather conspicuous by their absence in fig 49. In fact a double bottom is fitted above the LWL which runs on a full-length stringer each side.

Thus, including the bilge keels, there are longitudinals at between 15 and 18 in. centres and these in conjunction with various bulkheads and semi-bulkheads in way of seats and so forth have made for a pretty robust boat that has been working for some five years now without trouble.

Scuppers

On the subject, vaguely, of double bottoms it might be of interest to set out the Norwegian regulations for freeing ports. These state that when an open cockpit has its floor at least 35 cm ($13\frac{3}{4}$ in.) above the waterline of the fully equipped boat it should be self-baling. The total freeing area is not to be less than:

Area (cm^2) $= 40 + 15 \times$ area of cockpit sole (m^2).

Converted to Imperial units that could be written:

Area (sq. in.) $= 0.155 \times (40 + 1.4A)$ where A is the cockpit area in square feet.

Worked out that comes to quite formidable figures. If a cockpit was 2 m × 2 m (6.56 ft × 6.56 ft) the freeing area would have to be 100 sq. cm or 15.5 sq. in. That implies two drains each a little over 3 in. diameter or two drains each about 80 mm diameter. These are realistic figures for the self-draining characteristics of most cockpits are pitiful. Sailing boats usually have a starboard side cockpit drain leading out under the port bilge and vice versa so that when heeled inlet and outlet are not both under water. The same scheme can be adopted with motor boats but is not usual.

12 ft (3.6 m) ROWING/SAILING DINGHY

This is based on quite a successful design for a 15-footer I did a couple of years ago. That one has sold and is selling in satisfactory numbers so I don't think it would be fair to the builder to reproduce the lines and other details. In any case it was a G.R.P. boat and it might be of more interest here to have a go at something in foam sandwich.

The essence of this construction is that it is possible to turn out a lightish and very rigid boat with the low maintenance qualities of G.R.P. but without having to build first an exact replica of the required boat in wood (called the plug), subsequently taking an expensive mould off the plug before actually starting to lay-up the first real boat. With foam sandwich a batten mould is first made (fig 53), all rather as in cold-moulded timber construction; the foam is laid over this mould and secured in place (and even string will do for this, tying the foam down to the battens); the foam is then covered in the required number of

layers of resin and glass; the result so far is removed from the mould; foam is cut away down to the outer layer of resin and glass, in which cut-outs are laid in the framing; and the whole inside is then glassed over. It is unwise to lay framing directly on the foam and normally bulkheads, bunk fronts and so forth attached to glassed-over foam boundaries provide enough added stiffening. What hasn't been mentioned is the cleaning-off operation necessary outside to achieve a fair surface free of the inevitable humps and hollows left by the glassing. This is a tedious and time-consuming process and is the reason why professionally-built foam sandwich boats are never as cheap as one would hope.

On the dinghy shown the foam is laid on in diagonal strips. These should be reasonably well-fitting but the job is a quick one. On hard chine form the foam is normally used in sheets. Generally speaking, the expanded P.V.C. foams like Airex and Plasticell are employed where difficult and compound curves have to be covered. These can be heated in a primitive sort of oven with something like a hot-air hair dryer and when thus heated are pliable enough to be bent round most shapes. When they cool they take up their new curves without deformation or drop in mechanical strength. The expanded polyester foams are cheaper and most widely used on simpler forms.

Curve of Areas

Anyway, figs 50 and 51 show the profile and lines plan of the dinghy and on that lines plan is a curve below the centreline in plan view called 'curve of areas'. Well, this gives another check on the fairness of

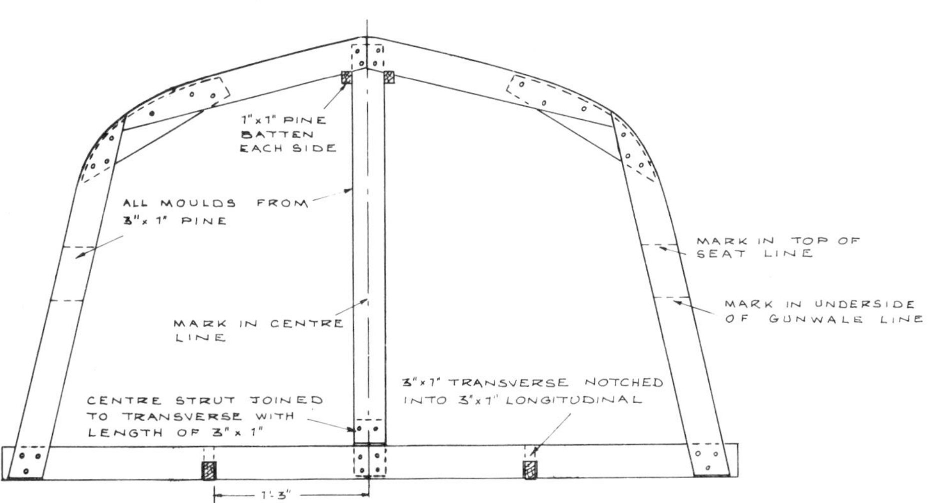

Fig 52 'midship building mould for the dinghy. These things can be built of scrap or unplaned timber

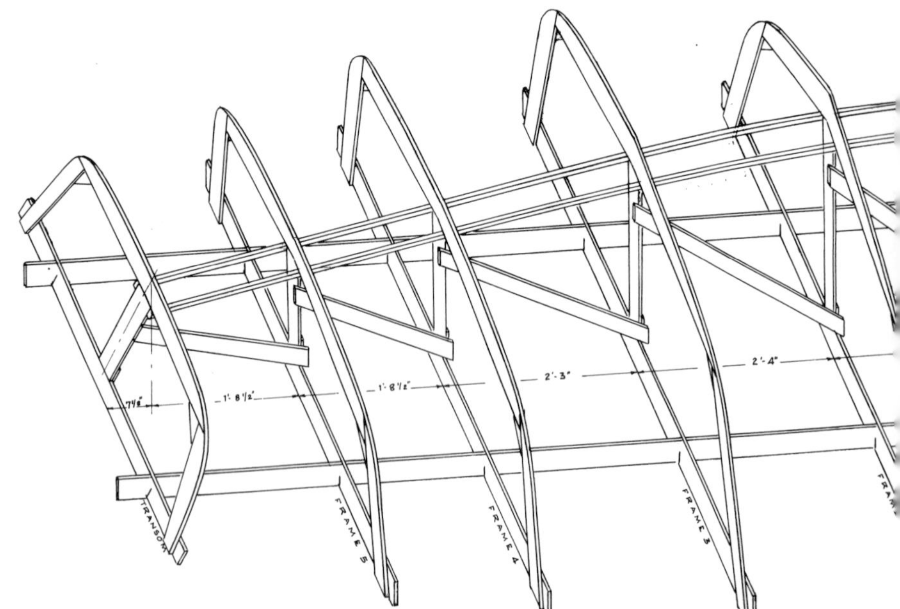

Fig 53 Various stages in building the dinghy. At the top the moulds are set up and, at the bottom, longitudinal battens are laid over them. On the battens diagonal strips of foam are bent as the core of the sandwich

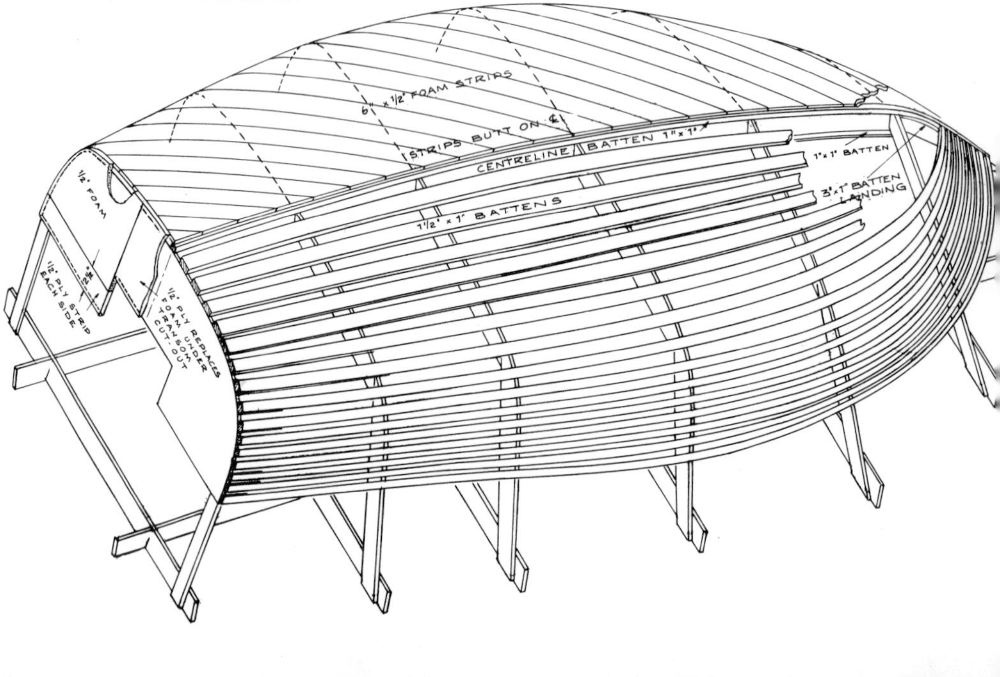

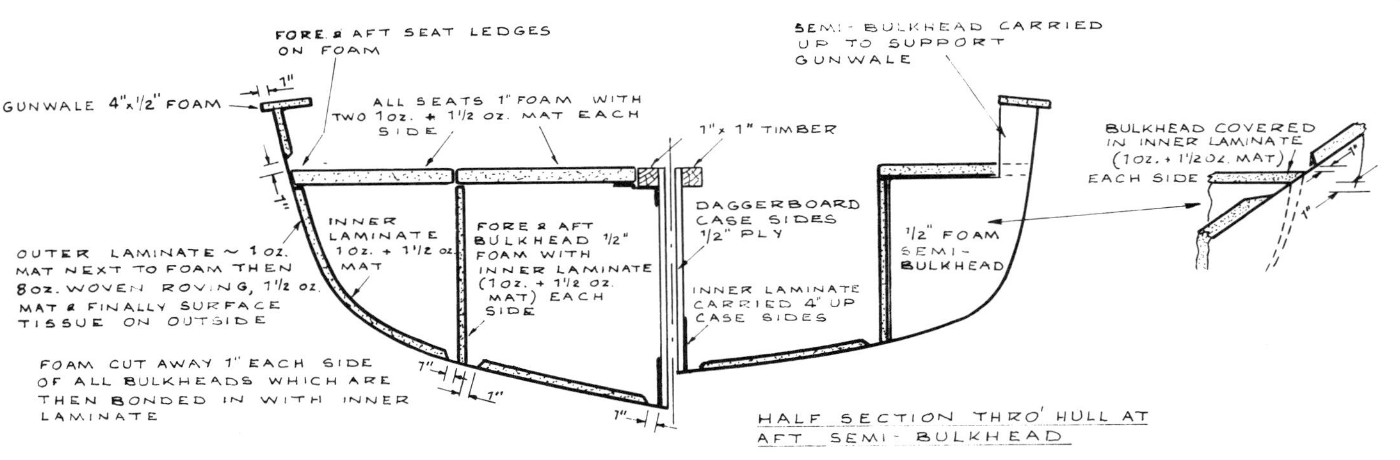

Fig 54 The structural 'midship section. It will be seen that all stiffening in the form of seats, bulkheads and so on, is arranged to land on the outer G.R.P. skin. The foam is cut away to this end

a hull. What one does is to plot the area of each section as a straight line along its station line. Thus, if an area (or half-area to be more precise) had been measured as, say 2.5 sq. ft mark a spot equal to 2.5, on whatever scale you are using, out from the centreline in plan view on the station line concerned. Thus, if the scale had been $1\frac{1}{2}$ in. $=1$ ft and the area was 2.5 sq. ft, the spot would be 2 ft 6 in. (the same thing as 2.5 ft) on $1\frac{1}{2}$ in. $=1$ ft scale out from the centreline. Now join the dots remembering that the curve will end at verticals down from LWL at both ends. If a fair curve can be drawn through the points you are in business. If it can't, check first on the area measurements for you might have made some small error that has thrown things out. If it is not that then you will have to contemplate redrawing the offending section(s) to obtain a more suitable area. Some people take this business rather seriously and probably they are right, but frankly I don't bother too much, though I would iron out any bad humps. The curve of areas was drawn here for another reason as well and that is to show how to obtain the displacement and LCB in one more way.

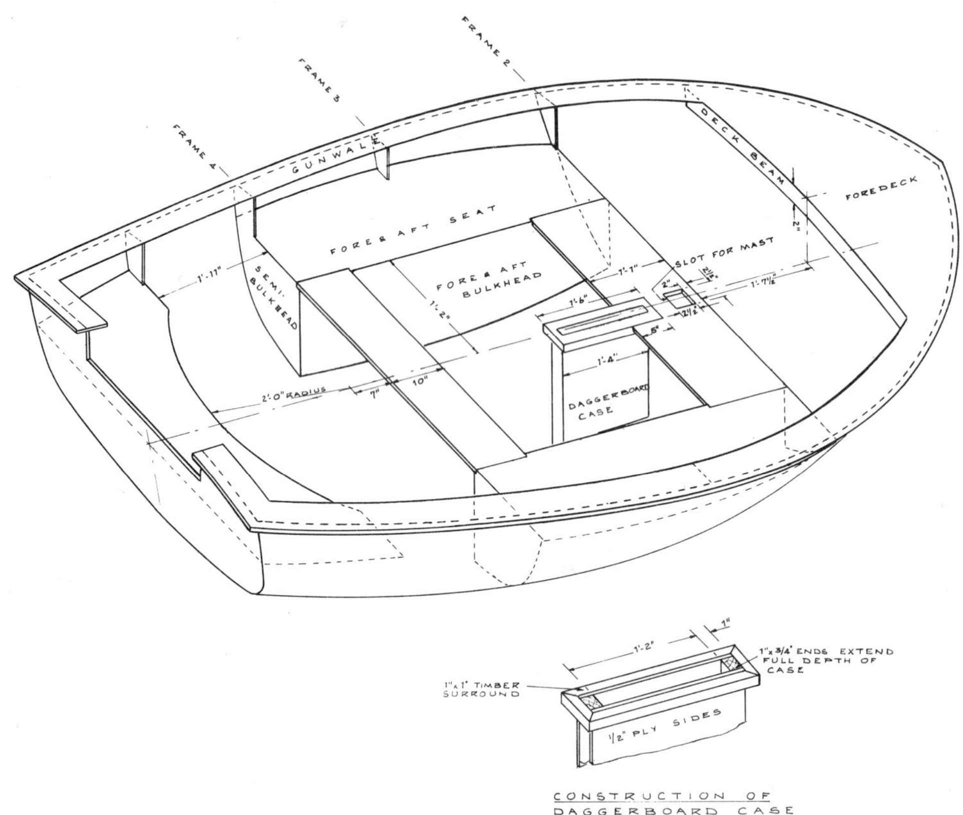

Fig 55 General layout of the dinghy

Displacement from Curve of Areas. As you will note, the stations are not equally spaced on the lines plan. This might happen because it is often useful on small boats to space the stations at where bulkheads or frames or something else occur when these are incorporated in the initial structure in place of, or supplementary to, the normal building moulds. So it is not now possible to use any of the calculations for displacement previously shown as they all relied on equally-spaced stations. A curve of areas is drawn and the area between that curve and the centreline is then measured—probably with a planimeter but it could be done by dividing into triangles and rectangles. Usually only half-areas have been taken so that the area will have to be doubled to give total displacement in cubic feet or metres or whatever. This is then converted to weight in the normal way and that is the displacement.

To obtain the LCB cut the curve outline and along the centreline; fold lengthways a few times to stiffen, and then balance on a compass point as was done when finding the CLR. The balancing point is the LCB.

There is only one further point to make here. If the forward sections of this lines plan and the previous one of fig 48 are compared it will be seen that above the waterline the sections of the bigger boat are hollow while on this one they are convex. Hollow sections above the water are excellent at throwing water clear of the boat in rough weather but on a dinghy which may well have someone sitting up forward they reduce the reserve buoyancy too much for comfort. On meeting a head sea the bow may not be able to lift because of its lack of buoyancy, and the wave will come aboard.

40 ft (12.19 m) KETCH

A few years ago I designed and saw to the building of the first of a class of motor yachts in Sweden. Having thoroughly enjoyed myself in pleasant surroundings and congenial company I was delighted to be asked a bit later to do the design of a 40-footer for the same people. This was to be a motor sailer and the profile of the resulting boat is shown in fig 56.

The lines are reproduced in fig 57 and I hope it will be obvious that the scheme was to turn out an easily driven yacht but one which would come into the motor sailer category by virtue of a large engine (this one had a diesel of around 80 hp) and moderate, easily-handled sail plan. The sail area/displacement ratio here is about 130 which puts it below the ratio average of 160 to 175 on waterline lengths of between 20 ft (6.09 m) and 40 ft (12.2 m). The lead of CE over CLR on this craft is 14.3 per cent of waterline length.

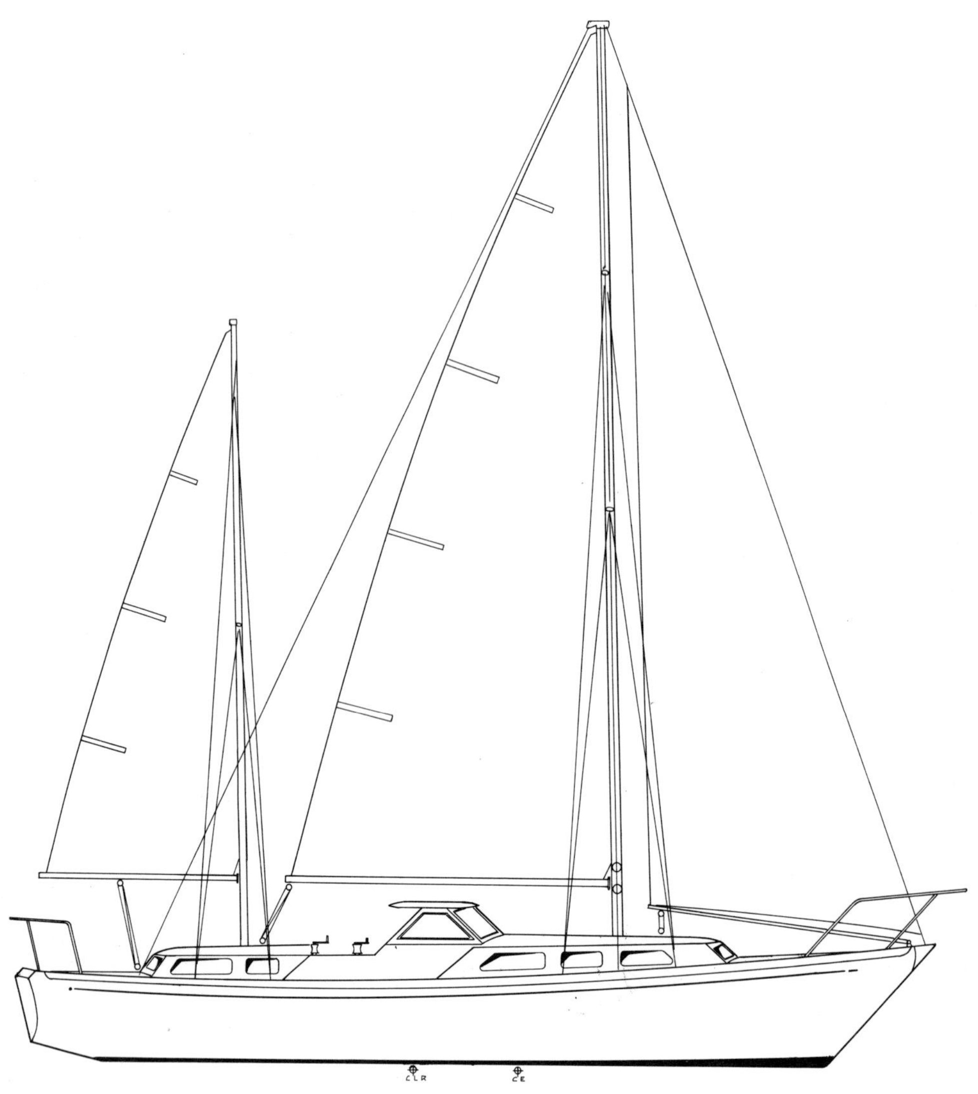

Fig 56 Swedish motor-sailer. LOA 40 ft (12.19 m); LWL 31 ft 2 in. (9.5 m); beam 12 ft (3.65 m); beam WL 10 ft 6 in. (3.2 m); draught 5 ft (1.5 m); LCB 0.5 ft (0.15 m) aft of 'midships; displacement 9.2 tons (9300 kilos); C_B 0.2; sail area 570 sq. ft (53 sq. m); sail area/displacement ratio 130

Prismatic Coefficient

Right at the beginning of the book we had a look at block coefficient which was the ratio of the immersed volume to the product of length, breadth and draught. Now we can deal with prismatic coefficient which is the ratio of the immersed volume to the area of the 'midship section multiplied by the waterline length. It can be written:

$$C_P = \frac{D \times 35}{A \times L}$$

where D is displacement and 35 is the multiplier to convert it to cubic feet of sea water. If using metric measurements the top line is in cubic metres as usual. A is the area in square feet (or square metres) of the 'midship section and L the waterline length in feet (or metres). For this yacht the sum would be:

$$C_P = \frac{9.2 \times 35}{20 \times 31.07} = 0.52$$

The longitudinal distribution of displacement is indicated by the value of this coefficient. Since the area of the 'midship section (immersed area that is) is on the bottom line, a low coefficient would suggest that on a given length and displacement the ends of a yacht were fine and the 'midship section full. A high C_P on the other hand would indicate a fine 'midship section and full ends.

So much for that and for many years prismatic coefficients for best performance were suggested for yachts based on a famous series of ship model tests. Note that these were ship and not yacht models. What C_P to adopt depends upon the speed/length ratio of the vessel and it was suggested that a figure of 0.58 was a good compromise for a fast cruising yacht. Since ours is 0.52 it would have meant that it was better suited to speed/length ratios of below 1.0 than for higher velocities. At maximum hull speeds the model tests showed that prismatics of 0.61 or so were required.

Anyway, what these suggestions did not take into account of was the effect of the keel on the yacht's C_P. If, for instance, there was a fin keel sited near 'midships this would lead to a concentration of area round 'midships which would reduce the prismatic coefficient. Other shapes and types of keel would also vary the C_P though the general hull shapes might be similar in all cases. To overcome this problem it was suggested that only the main body of the hull be considered in the calculation but this was obviously unsatisfactory since different designers would be bound to have different ideas of what constituted the main body. There would be no problems on a genuine fin-keeler where a plate is stuck under a canoe hull and a lump of ballast attached to it. It is where a keel is faired into a hull, as in this example, that difficulties arise.

Eventually an American designer, J. E. Paris, from a study of numerous successful designs developed a curve showing the best relationship between prismatic coefficient and lateral plane coefficient which overcame many of the inherent difficulties of using C_P on its own. Table 11 gives the broad outline of his suggestions with C_P ratios based on the C_{LP}.

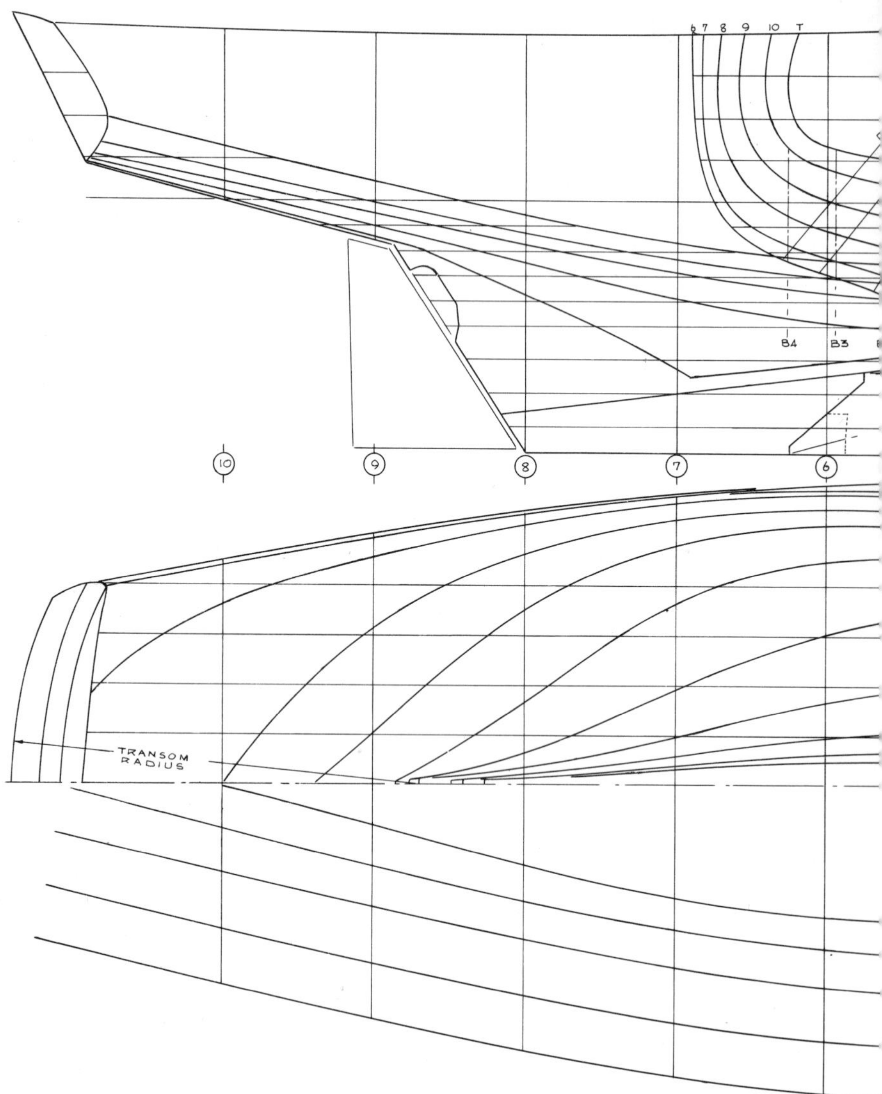

Fig 57 Lines plan of the 40 ft motor sailer. The forward bottom edge of the keel in profile should be well rounded for least resistance and the more it can be swept back as well the better will be performance

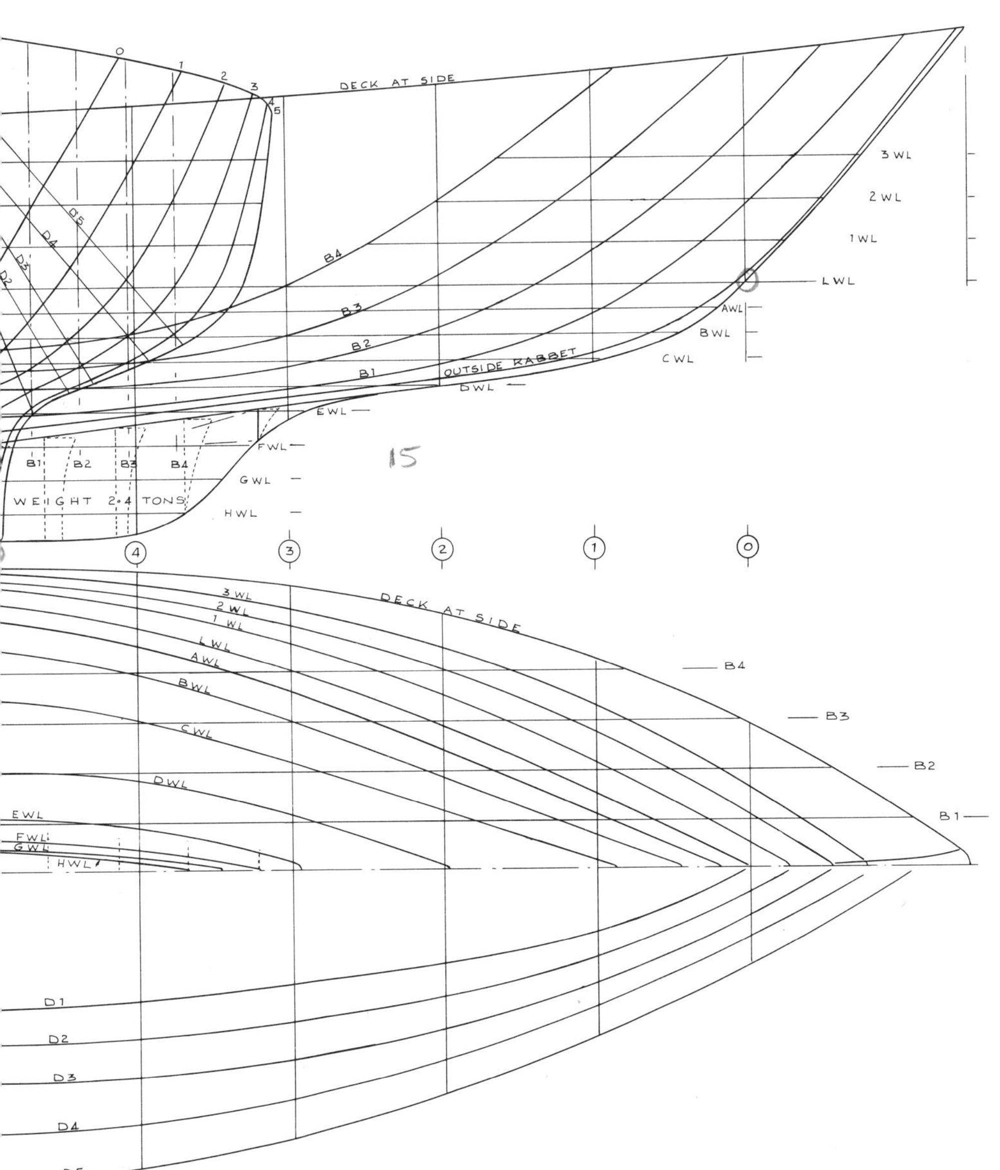
DECK AT SIDE
0
1
2
3
4
5
3 WL
2 WL
1 WL
LWL
AWL
BWL
CWL
DWL
EWL
FWL
GWL
HWL
OUTSIDE RABBET
B4
B3
B2
B1
D5
D4
D3
D2
WEIGHT 2·4 TONS
15
4
3
2
1
0
DECK AT SIDE
3 WL
2 WL
1 WL
LWL
AWL
BWL
CWL
DWL
EWL
FWL
GWL
HWL
B4
B3
B2
B1
D1
D2
D3
D4
D5

Lateral Plane Coefficient (C_{LP})

This is the ratio of the projected area of the lateral plane to the circumscribing rectangle. In other words, it is the lateral plane area (the area of the underwater profile as used in the CLR business) divided by the product of waterline length and maximum draught. The 40-footer, using a metric scale for a change, works out like this:

Lateral plane area = 9.43 sq. m
Length × draught = 9.5 × 1.5 = 14.25 sq. m

$$\text{Lateral plane coefficient} = \frac{9.43}{14.25} = 0.66$$

If we have a look at table 11 now, it will be seen that for such a coefficient the recommended prismatic coefficient will be somewhere between 0.51 and 0.53. Since ours worked out at 0.52 all should be well.

Angles of Entrance and Exit

I'm not quite sure that there is such a thing as an angle of exit but if the angle the LWL makes with the centreline at its fore end is called the angle of entrance, perhaps the same waterline's angle with the centreline at the stern could be called the angle of exit?

Still, it doesn't matter what the name is as long as we know what we are talking about. In fact we are really discussing half-angles, the angle between the load waterline and centreline that you would measure off your lines plan, as only one side of the boat has been drawn. This half-angle forward should be between 20 and 25 degrees—on the motor sailer it is 25 degrees—and the lines should be kept either straight or slightly convex. Hollow load waterlines are not a very good scheme. Aft, the half-angle should be between 35 and 50 degrees and ours is, in fact, 50 degrees. The beamier the boat the greater those half-angles inevitably are.

One more point about waterlines. It is important to keep the waterlines at the top of the keel, EWL and FWL on the lines plan reproduced, as fine as practical. A blunt-nosed entry here can increase resistance quite considerably. All these suggestions are for genuine cruising boats but where a degree of speed is desired. They do not necessarily apply to modern racing craft about which, I must confess, I know very little.

Longitudinal Centre of Buoyancy

Fast cruising boats, which this one would be with a bit more sail, should have their LCB's between 52 and 54 per cent of the waterline length aft of the forward LWL ending. Here it is 52 per cent.

That leads us on to the subject of ballasting and ballast keels, plus ballast keel bolts. We can stick all this lot under a general heading.

Ballast

As the ballast keel on the motor sailer weighs 2.4 tons and the total displacement is 9.2 tons, the ballast ratio is $\frac{2.4}{9.2} \times 100 = 26.1$ per cent. On a beamy motor sailer with quite restricted sail area this is sufficient for nobody is likely to buy this boat with the intention of racing to windward in a gale. Rather, sail would be reduced and the motor switched on when conditions became too uncomfortable. For more serious cruising under sail the ballast ratio could be increased to about 35 per cent. It is unrealistic to aim for a very high ratio on a cruising boat where the weight of stores and general odds and ends accumulated during the season (and for which a guess should be made in the weights calculation) may be considerable.

It is sensible to allow a certain amount for final trimming ballast. Weight added or subtracted in the stern for example, can have a significant effect on a yacht's performance but only sailing trials will reveal the facts. A professional designer might allow 5 per cent of the total ballast weight to be in the form of movable inside ballast but an amateur had better allow rather more. Ten per cent should be about right and this will also allow him a margin for error in the calculations!

Whether lead or iron is used for the ballast keel is largely a matter of design. If a tiny fin keel is slung below the hull and a good ballast ratio required, lead will have to be used for iron would take up too much room and probably not allow the weight to be concentrated sufficiently far down. On the other hand, if there is plenty of room for the ballast keel, iron is cheaper than lead and adds strength to a boat. Though both their weights are given at the beginning of the book it might be worth repeating here that iron weighs about 450 lb/cu. ft and lead 710 lb/cu. ft (7200 kilos per cu. m and 11 350 kilos per cu. m respectively).

LCG of Ballast Keel. The method of finding the desired centre of gravity of the keel was explained in the last chapter and it is exactly the same here. However, this keel is rather an odd shape and so we have to find its area and LCG exactly as if we were doing a displacement calculation. Table 12 shows the working for this boat and the dotted sections on the keel of fig 57 show the seven sections used in the sums. As can be seen, the area was 11.9 cu. ft which gives about 2.4 tons of cast iron. An additional 0.1 tons was allowed for trimming purposes. Unhappily there is no short way around this work. All one can do after finding where the required LCG lies is to guess a shape and see whether its area and centre of gravity correspond with that required.

Electrolytic Action

Having achieved a ballast keel it must be fastened to the hull, and this brings up the selection of keel bolt material. Table 13 shows the galvanic series. To some extent the positioning of the metals in the table depends upon their specification but this is generally correct for most commercially available metals. Sea water being an admirable electrolyte, two dissimilar metals under water tend to form a cell with current flowing from one to the other; from those forming the positive electrode of the cell to those acting as the negative electrode. The metals in table 13 are arranged in an order known as electro-chemical series with the noble, or negative metals at the top. These will attack those lower down in the series and eat them away. Thus, if you put iron fastenings on a copper-sheathed boat, the iron being quite a long way below copper in the series would be destroyed. The table is also the explanation for zinc sacrificial plates put on the bottom near rudders, propellers and shafts. Zinc, being the least noble of all practical metals is eaten away before any other metal.

When it comes to keel bolts through an iron or lead keel, we need to consult the table. The practical materials would seem to be stainless steel (which might attack the iron or lead but there is so much metal in a ballast keel that this would not matter in practice); naval brass; one of the bronzes; or gunmetal. Stainless steel is rather suspect under water being prone to crevice or stress corrosion where it becomes pitted and weakened. Naval brass is good but not very easy to get hold of; the bronze alloys are liable to de-zincification in the case of manganese bronze and de-aluminisation in the case of aluminium bronze; and gunmetal is not all that strong. If we look below iron or lead in the table we find aluminium alloy (which would be attacked by the keel material and probably every other metal along the bottom as well); and galvanised mild steel where the galvanising which is zinc would be eaten away to leave bare mild steel. So the problem is a difficult one and probably best served by using ordinary mild steel and either getting it red hot and then plunging it into tar (sometimes called Chinese galvanising) or coating it very thoroughly with an epoxy paint.

One further point . . . though stainless steel is right at the top of the noble end of the table it can be used in proximity to most other metals without problems. In fact, it is often employed to fasten aluminium alloys with complete success. Looking at the table you would not expect this and would say that galvanised steel or, of course, aluminium alloy fastenings would be better. Above water those two would be good but below the surface they are likely to be attacked by all other metals, whereas stainless is not. Obviously though, a copper or brass fastening in an aluminium fitting would be a disaster since it would attack the alloy. Remember that bulk counts. You can afford to lose a bit of ballast keel by electrolytic attack but you cannot afford to lose any metal from the bolts themselves.

Timber Construction

There are various methods of planking available to round bilge boats apart from the usual carvel and clinker systems. Fig 58 illustrates a few

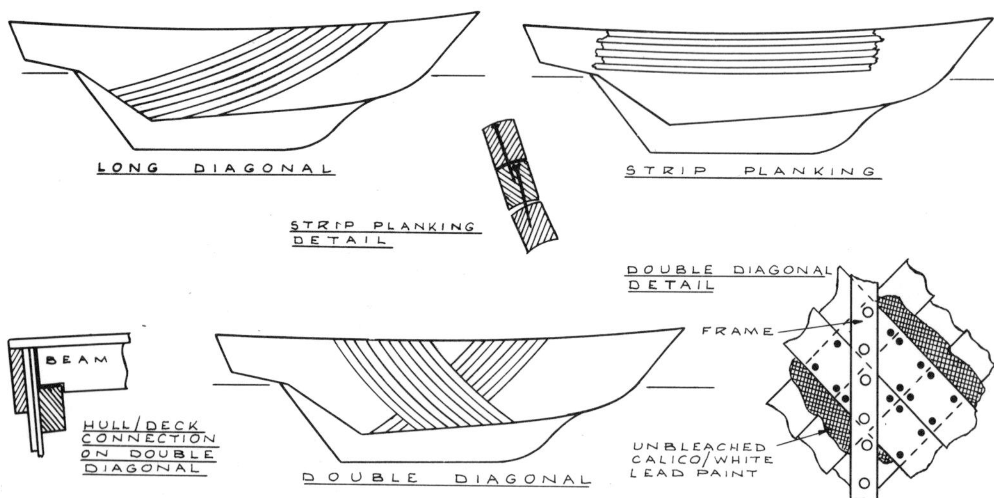

Fig 58 As an alternative to conventional carvel, or possibly clinker, planking any of these three methods may be used on a round-bilge boat

of them. The top left-hand sketch shows the long diagonal, single-skin scheme which was nearly specified on this motor sailer. The advantage is that comparatively short lengths of timber are needed and it is usually possible to avoid butts in the planking. Normally the planks are edge-glued and not caulked and though this sounds like a lot of work, in fact it is simple enough. What is done is to put the first plank in parallel-sided and all subsequent strakes are butted, temporarily fastened or clamped and a spindle run up the joint. This cuts away the wood so that the edges can be pushed together as a perfect fit.

The only problem comes at the deck where, because the planking is running up diagonally, all the top edges show end grain which gives a poor hold for the deck edge fastenings. Consequently it is usual to fit a strake outside the planking as in the bottom left-hand sketch, which shows the scheme for double diagonal planking where the same problem occurs.

Strip Planking, right-hand top sketch, is also a quick method of construction since the narrow strakes can normally be pushed into position without any shaping. Though Lloyds require the planks to be shaped in section as shown, many amateurs simply use straight-edged timber and bevel as they go. The strakes are glued and edge-nailed together, and the whole, if well carried out, makes for a strong structure. Like all glued systems, repairs tend to be rather difficult.

Double Diagonal planking is shown along the bottom of fig 58. This is an ancient and honoured method and Lloyds allow a reduction in planking thickness of 10 per cent if it is employed—just as they do with cold moulded and clinker building. A ply skin rates a 25 per cent reduction, but that is another story. With double diagonal there are clearly gaps at each crossing point of the two skins which is why there must be a layer of waterproof material between them. Unbleached calico is the traditional filling to the sandwich, coated with a white lead paint mixture which should still be wet when the outer layer of planking is applied. If this is so the calico will stay in good condition, and keep the water out, for many years. The substitution of varnish for white lead is a step in the wrong direction.

Fig 59 shows various details of the construction of the 40-footer. Note the heavier frames that are used in way of the masts and the hanging knees which help tie the structure together in the same area. The engine beds are specified as pine because a softwood tends to dampen out vibration better than a hardwood. In the deadwood area at the back end of the keel a bolt through a floor is shown apparently ending in nothing. What happens here is that the timber is chiselled away from one side sufficiently to allow a nut and washer to be placed over the bolt. The bolt is tightened and the hole left by the chiselling plugged. This scheme is common enough when there are big baulks of wood to be joined. All joints are resorcinal-glued. The gunwale is a rather unusual construction and I can't remember why it was done this way except that the builders requested it. Obviously they had a reason for it is standard procedure on all their craft. A radiused transom like the one shown usually has an inner skin of ply with an outer layer of planking, vertical or horizontal, depending upon which the owner thinks would look best.

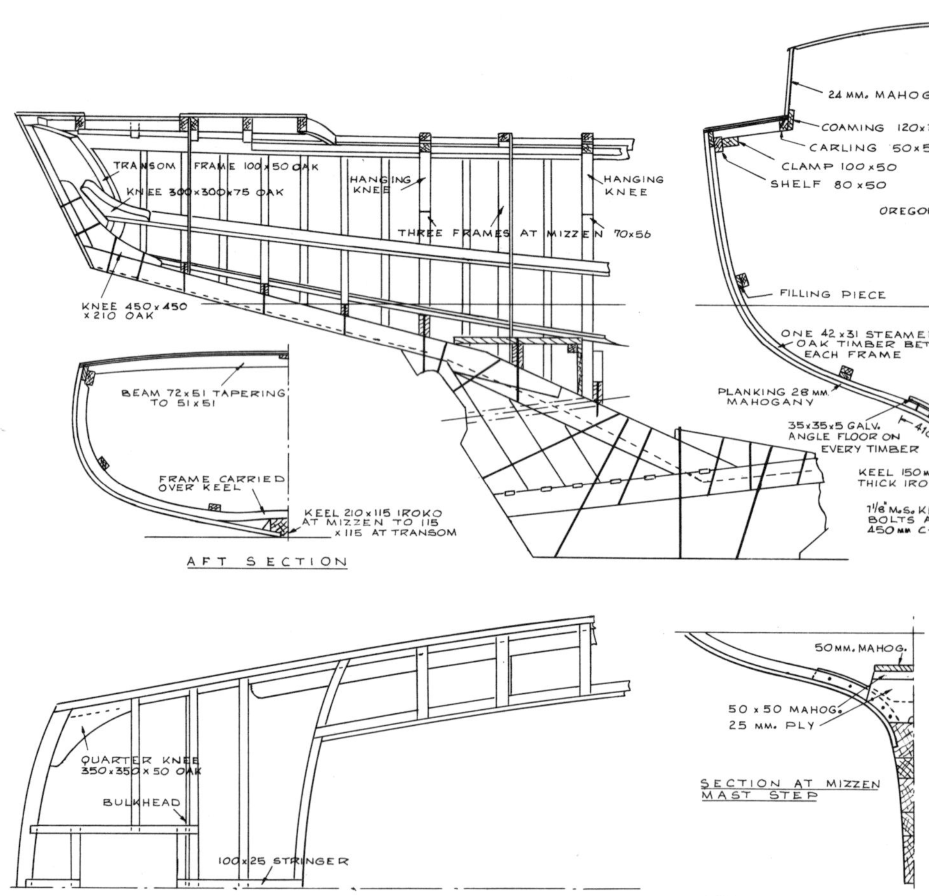

Fig 59 Constructional details of the motor sailer. If the stringers run on diagonals, as they do here, the diagonals must be specified

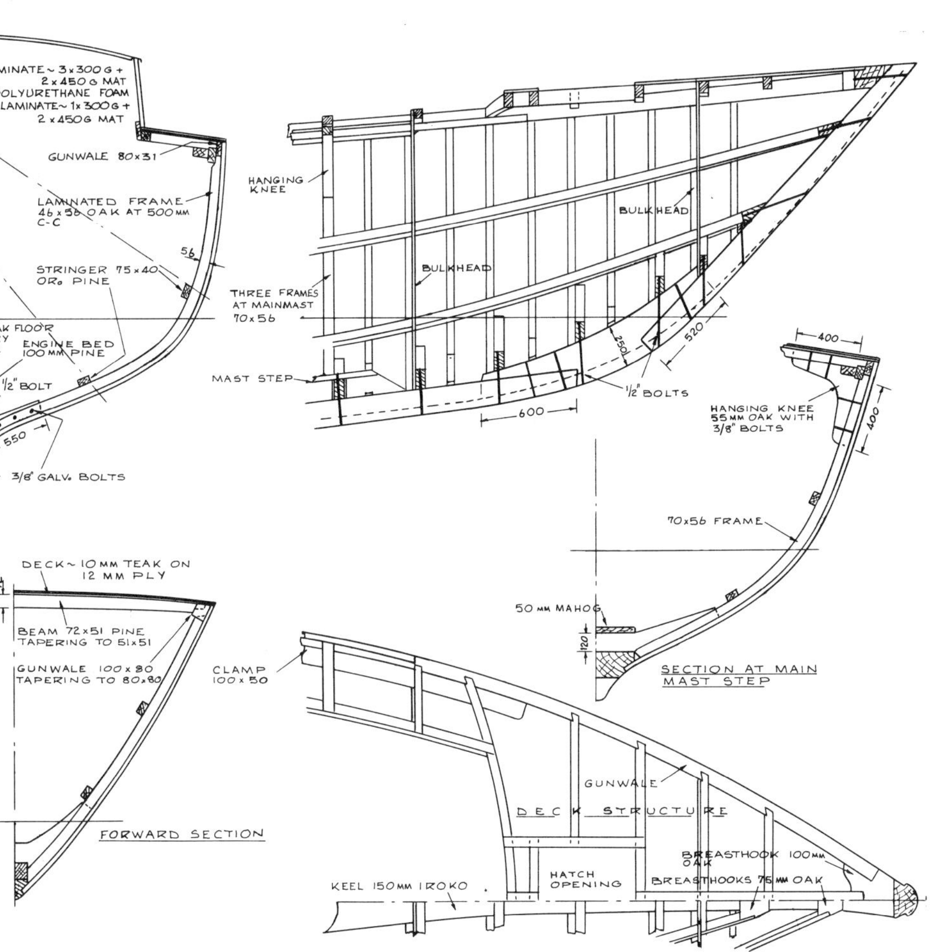
MINATE ~ 3 x 300 G +
2 x 450 G MAT
OLYURETHANE FOAM
LAMINATE ~ 1 x 300 G +
2 x 450 G MAT
GUNWALE 80 x 31
LAMINATED FRAME
46 x 58 OAK AT 500 MM
C-C
56
STRINGER 75 x 40
OR. PINE
AK FLOOR
ENGINE BED
100 MM PINE
1/2" BOLT
550
3/8" GALV. BOLTS
HANGING KNEE
THREE FRAMES AT MAINMAST 70 x 56
MAST STEP
BULKHEAD
BULKHEAD
250
520
600
1/2" BOLTS
400
400
HANGING KNEE 55 MM OAK WITH 3/8" BOLTS
70 x 56 FRAME
50 MM MAHOG
120
SECTION AT MAIN MAST STEP
DECK ~ 10 MM TEAK ON 12 MM PLY
BEAM 72 x 51 PINE TAPERING TO 51 x 51
GUNWALE 100 x 80 TAPERING TO 80 x 80
CLAMP 100 x 50
FORWARD SECTION
GUNWALE
DECK STRUCTURE
BREASTHOOK 100 MM OAK
HATCH OPENING
BREASTHOOKS 75 MM OAK
KEEL 150 MM IROKO

Fig 60 Details of the spacing of butts in conventional planking and the various methods of making butt and scarph joints

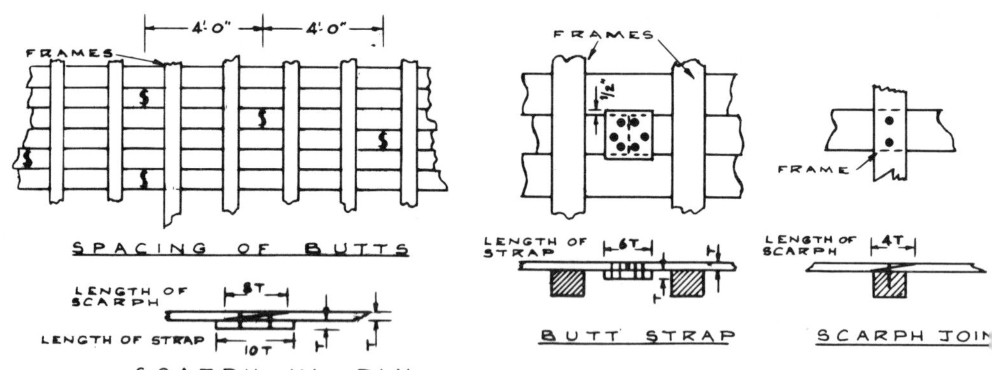

Butts and Scarphs. A few more general details are shown in fig 60; butt joints must be staggered and scarphs can be substituted but they should be made using a frame as backing. Lloyds say that if a scarph joint in ply is made on the job, rather than on the bench, then a strap must be fitted behind it. Its dimensions are shown. My own feeling is that only the very skilled can make an accurate scarph in ply and that a simple butt is often preferable. In that case the width of butt strap should be about 24 times the thickness of the ply being joined for $\frac{1}{4}$ in. (6 mm) ply; 20 times for $1\frac{1}{2}$ in. (12 mm) ply; and 15 times the thickness for 1 in. (25 mm) ply. In all cases its thickness would be the same as the ply sheet and it, too, would be made of ply.

Fig 61 concerns itself with stems and shows two ways of making one from timber. Stopwaters are also shown and these are softwood dowels that are driven in at jointing surfaces. When wet they will swell and help prevent water creeping in along those joints. The terms rabbet and back rabbet are illustrated, though back rabbet is an infrequent bit of terminology. All the lines that have been shown in this book have been drawn to the outside of planking, which is the conventional way of doing things, and so we have been talking about plain or outside rabbets (fig 57).

Balance

Actually I had not intended to write about hull balance at all for it is a subject fraught with theories, methods and discussion but without, as far as I know, any definite conclusions. However, it seems that everyone else has a go at the business and so, with some foreboding, here is my offering.

The problem is straightforward enough and can be divided into two bits. The first is that since the centre of effort of the sail plan is nearly always ahead of the centre of gravity (or area) of the waterplane its effect is to push the bows down and so cause asymmetric heeling.

Fig 61 Two methods of stem construction. A third would be to laminate the whole thing

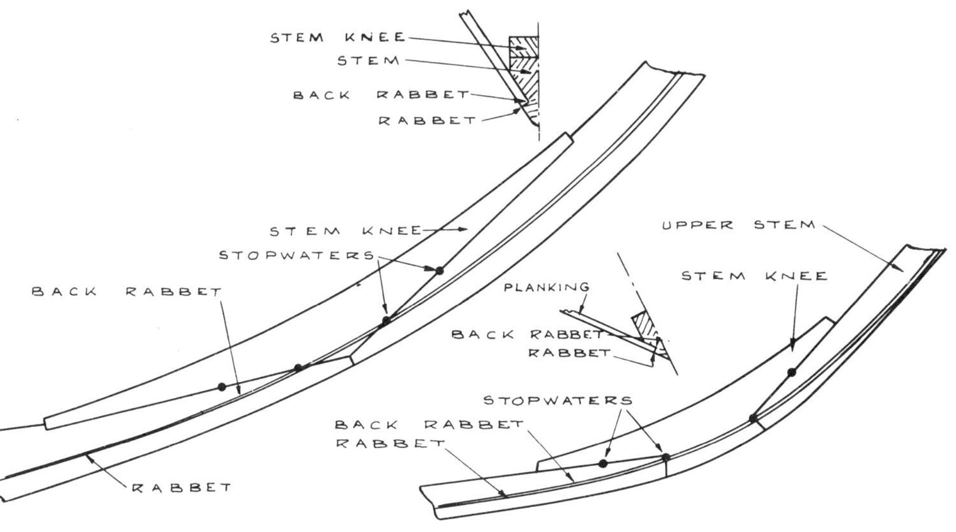

Secondly, and if you look at fig 62 this argument might be clearer, as a boat heels the wedge shaped areas that are immersed are in almost every case of greater area than those wedge-shaped sections that emerge. The difference in the two areas will vary through the length of the craft. Because a boat must always have the same volume beneath the waterline, simply because its displacement cannot alter, it will lift or sink and trim by the bow or stern until the immersed and emerged areas are the same.

Whatever its upright waterline, therefore, its shape when heeled will be completely altered and is almost impossible to predict. The consequence is that a vessel that was balanced and easy on the helm in light airs may develop totally different characteristics when heeled over in a good breeze.

Metacentric Shelf. This question of hull balance came to the fore in yachting circles in about 1937 when Engineer-Admiral Alfred Turner put forward a method of organising hull balance on a yacht such that 'when heeled to a substantial angle her immersed body lies symmetrically about a vertical plane that is parallel to the original amidships line'. This was called the Metacentric Shelf theory and the Shelf was defined as the middle line of the trough made by the heeled immersed body. The amounts the centre of gravity of the various sections of the underwater hull lay to one side or other of this reference plane were plotted. If the moment areas at the bow and stern were equal and in sum totalled the 'midships area the boat was considered balanced. I put all that down, not because it explains the detailed method of doing the job but to illustrate how complex the subject can become. Anyway, the theory behind the calculations was said to be wrong by the brains of the day, though it worked quite well in practice. Unfortunately it tended to produce craft with fairly symmetrical waterline shapes fore and aft of 'midships which in turn made for rather slow vessels.

Since then the metacentric shelf method has been dropped and others have taken its place but as it quite often happens that a boat unbalanced by theory in fact sails very well, and vice versa, obviously there is still a lot to be learned.

There is one quite simple check that can be made over potential hull balance and the method is shown in fig 62. Draw, say, three heeled waterlines with one at near the greatest angle possible before the deck edge becomes immersed. Distances are taken from the sectional view and plotted on the plan view to give the waterplane shape. Now cut out tracing paper patterns of these plus that of the LWL, fold lengthways a few times and balance each on a compass point. The balancing position is the centre of area (or gravity) of the waterplane concerned. Prick these points through and transfer them to the plan view. The spots marked WPCG (waterplane centre of gravity) are the ones we are talking about. For a boat to be potentially a balanced sailer the centres of gravity should not shift more than about 3 per cent of the waterline length forward or aft of the centre of gravity of the upright LWL. In the case of the motor sailer illustrated the maximum shift (between 28 degrees WPCG and LWLCG) is $2\frac{1}{2}$ per cent. Though this cannot be said to be a 100 per cent guarantee of superior performance under sail it is a useful check.

As will also be seen the CE has been marked and this is some $7\frac{1}{2}$ per cent of the waterline length forward of LWLCG. I wouldn't want a greater distance than that and less would be better but difficult to achieve on this boat.

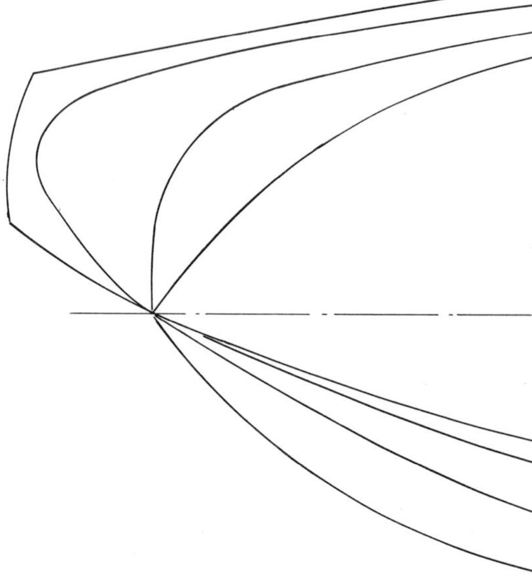

Fig 62 If a heeled waterplane is drawn on the sections of a lines plan, using the buttock lines in profile will enable the tricky bit of the waterplane in plan—right aft—to be drawn. This will become obvious when you look at the problem, but is difficult to explain

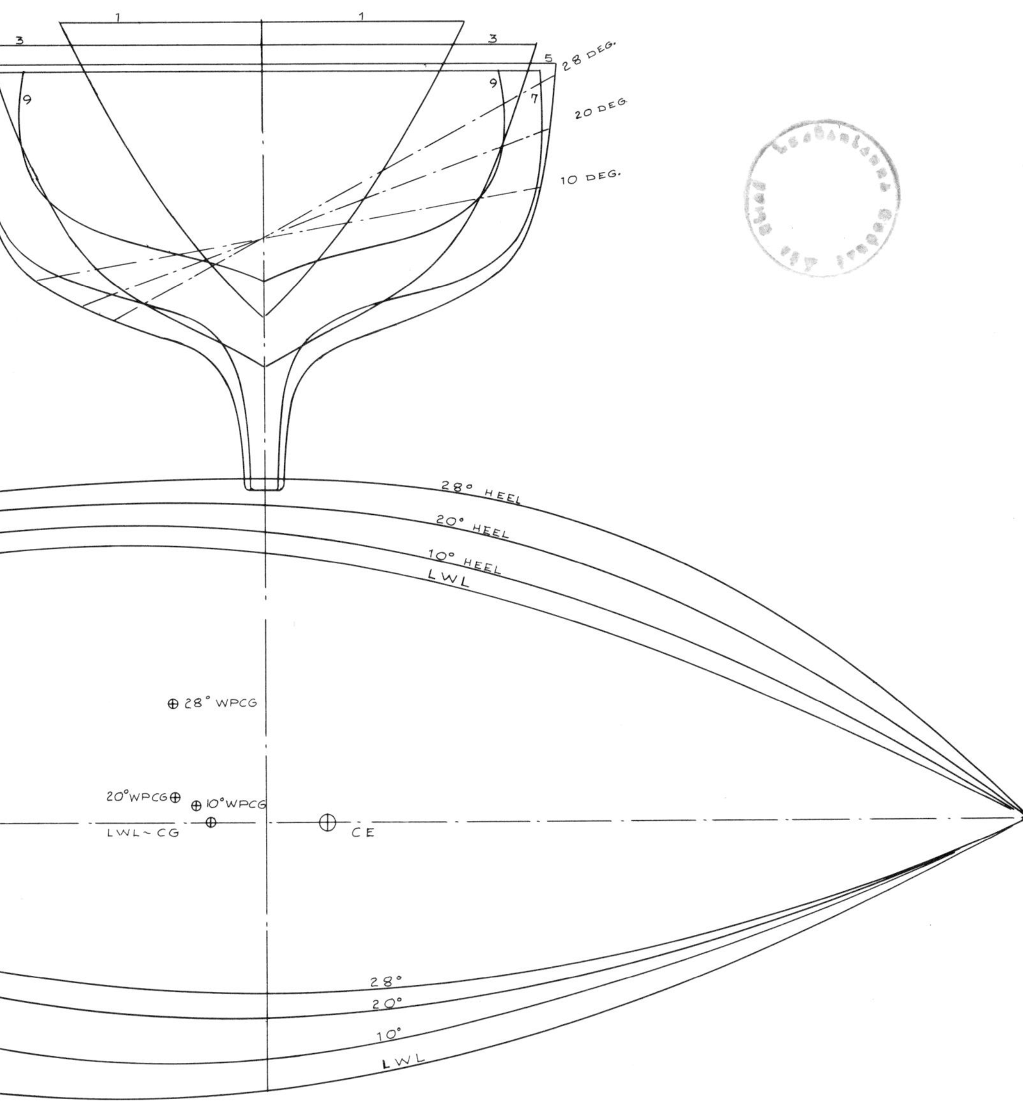

5. Tables

TABLE 1

Weight Calculation for 29 ft Flattie

Hull and cabin 5 sheets $\frac{3}{8}$ in. (9 mm) ply	=	198 lb
24 sheets $\frac{1}{4}$ in. (6 mm) ply	=	530
		728
Framing can be taken as $\frac{1}{3}$ weight of ply	=	242
So add to the two totals		970
Spars, sails, ironwork, fastenings, paint	=	300
That was a guess but add it in		1270
Stores, outboard, fuel, bedding, water	=	250
Another guess but keep adding		1520
Four people at 150 lb each		600
Call that final total a ton (2240 lb)		2120 lb

TABLE 2

Displacement and LCB Calculation for 29 ft Flattie

Station	Area (sq. ft)	Multiplier	Product (1)	Lever	Product (2)
0	—	1	—	4	—
1	0.40	4	1.60	3	4.80
2	1.05	2	2.10	2	4.20
3	1.51	4	6.04	1	6.04
4	1.57	2	3.14	–	15.04
5	1.36	4	5.44	1	5.44
6	0.93	2	1.86	2	3.72
7	0.47	4	1.88	3	5.64
8	—	1	—	4	—
			22.06		14.80

Common Interval (station spacing) is 2.83 ft = CI

$$\text{Displacement} = \frac{2}{3} \times \text{CI} \times \frac{\text{Product total (1)}}{35} = \frac{2}{3} \times 2.83 \times \frac{22.06}{35} = 1.2 \text{ tons}$$

$$\text{LCB} = \frac{\text{Difference in product (2) totals}}{\text{product (1) total}} \times \text{CI} = \frac{(15.04 - 14.80)}{22.06} \times 2.83 = 0.028 \text{ ft}$$

Since the total products for the forward sections were greater than for the aft sections the LCB is 0.028 ft forward of station 4. That is about $\frac{5}{16}$ in.

TABLE 3

Dinghy Performance Coefficients

	12 ft Nat.	14 ft Int.	14 ft Merlin	16 ft Hornet	17 ft Canoe	18 ft Skiff	20 ft FD	29 ft Black Soo	38 ft Scow
Disp. Coeff. $\frac{D}{(\frac{L}{100})^3}$	145	98	105	75	32	86	39	90	33
Sail Area Coeff. $\frac{SA}{D^{\frac{2}{3}}}$	253	332	276	284	360	600	423	215	560

Notes:
FD is Flying Dutchman;

the Canoe is the 17 ft International sailing canoe;

the 18 ft Skiff is the Australian/New Zealand Sydney Harbour type and is setting main and large working jib;

Black Soo is a Van de Stadt chine ocean racer, displacement 1.57 tons;

the 38 ft Scow is a Class A Inland Lake Scow from the U.S.A.;

D is displacement in tons;

L for dinghies is generally overall length in feet and for the bigger craft, waterline length.

TABLE 4

Displacement and LCB Rigid Bottom Inflatable

Station	Area sq. ft	Simpson's Multiplier	Product	Lever	Product
0	0.1	1	0.1	5	0.5
1	0.68	4	2.72	4	10.88
2	0.97	2	1.94	3	5.84
3	1.13	4	4.52	2	9.04
4	1.23	2	2.46	1	2.46
5	1.34	4	5.36	–	28.72
6	1.36	2	2.72	1	2.72
7	1.39	4	5.56	2	11.12
8	1.37	2	2.74	3	8.22
9	1.35	4	5.40	4	21.60
10	1.33	1	1.33	5	6.65
			34.85		50.31

Correction for $1\frac{1}{2}$ in. = 1 ft scale: $34.85 \times \frac{4}{9} = 15.5$ sq. ft

Displacement $= 15.5 \times \frac{2}{3} \times 1.125 \times 64 = 745$ lb (station spacing = 1.125 ft)

$$\text{LCB} = \frac{50.31 - 28.72}{34.85} \times 1.125 = 1.025 \text{ ft aft station 5}$$

Displacement and LCB 40 ft (12 m) Yacht

Station	Area sq. m	Simpson's Multiplier	Product	Lever	Product
0	—	1	—	5	—
1	0.00053	4	0.00212	4	0.00848
2	0.00135	2	0.00270	3	0.00810
3	0.00245	4	0.00980	2	0.01960
4	0.00382	2	0.00764	1	0.00764
5	0.00443	4	0.01772	–	0.04382
6	0.00400	2	0.00800	1	0.00800
7	0.00281	4	0.01124	2	0.02248
8	0.00163	2	0.00326	3	0.00978
9	0.00036	4	0.00144	4	0.00576
10	—	1	—	5	—
			0.06392		0.04602

Correction for 1.15 scale: $0.06392 \times 225 = 14.4$

Displacement $= \frac{2}{3} \times 0.965 \times 14.4 = 9.3$ cu. m or 9.3 tonnes (station spacing 0.965 m)

$$\text{LCB} = \frac{0.04602 - 0.04382}{0.06392} \times 0.965 = 0.0333 \text{ m aft station 5}$$

TABLE 5

Offset Table for Rigid Bottom Inflatable

Station	0	1	2	3	4	5	6	7	8	9	Transom
HALF-BREADTHS FROM ℄											
W.L. 1		0–2–6	0–5–0	0–6–0	0–6–5	0–6–7	0–6–7	0–6–4	0–5–4	0–4–3	
2		0–5–6	0–9–0	0–10–7	1–0–1	1–1–1	1–2–0	1–2–4	1–2–7	1–3–1	1–3–3
3	0–1–3	0–9–4	1–1–3	1–3–5	1–5–4	1–7–3	1–8–7	1–10–3	1–11–3	2–0–2	2–0–6
4	0–4–4	1–1–6	1–6–4	1–9–0	1–11–3	2–1–5	2–4–0				
5	0–8–1	1–6–7	2–0–3	2–3–0							
6	1–1–0										
Deck at Side and Knuckle	1–7–2	2–2–1	2–4–4	2–4–6	2–4–7	2–5–0	2–5–1	2–5–3	2–5–4	2–5–5	2–5–6
℄ Tube on Deck	1–0–6	1–8–7	1–11–3	1–11–5	1–11–7	2–0–0	2–0–1	2–0–2	2–0–4	2–0–5	2–0–6
HEIGHTS ABOVE BASE											
Keel	0–11–5	0–5–7	0–5–1	0–5–0	0–5–1	0–5–3	0–5–6	0–6–0	0–6–3	0–6–5	0–6–7
Buttock 1	1–1–4	0–6–3	0–5–4	0–5–2	0–5–3	0–5–5	0–5–7	0–6–0	0–6–3	0–6–5	0–6–7
2	1–3–3	0–7–6	0–6–2	0–6–0	0–5–7	0–5–7	0–6–1	0–6–3	0–6–5	0–6–7	0–6–7
3	1–6–5	0–11–4	0–9–1	0–8–0	0–7–5	0–7–3	0–7–2	0–7–3	0–7–4	0–7–5	0–7–6
4	1–9–4	1–2–5	0–11–7	0–10–4	0–9–6	0–9–2	0–9–0	0–9–0	0–9–0	0–9–0	0–9–0
5	2–0–2	1–6–3	1–3–5	1–2–1	1–1–0	1–0–2	0–11–5	0–11–2	0–10–7	0–10–7	0–10–7
6											
Knuckle	2–0–5	1–9–7	1–8–4	1–7–5	1–6–5	1–5–5	1–4–4	1–3–4	1–3–0	1–2–5	1–2–5
Deck at Side	2–2–6	2–0–0	1–10–5	1–9–5	1–9–1	1–9–0	1–8–7	1–8–5	1–8–4	1–8–3	1–8–2
DIAGONALS											
Diagonal 1	0–3–1	0–8–3	0–10–1	0–11–0	0–11–3	0–11–4	0–11–4	0–11–3	0–11–1	0–11–0	
2	2–2–3	2–4–7	2–10–3	2–11–5	3–0–5	3–1–3	3–2–0	3–2–3	3–2–5	3–2–6	

All dimensions in feet, inches, and eighths to outside of moulding.

TABLE 6

Displacement and LCB 16 ft Catamaran

Station	Area sq. ft	Distance from station 4	Product
0	0.06	6.0	0.36
1	0.27	4.5	1.21
2	0.45	3.0	1.35
3	0.51	1.5	0.76
4	0.61	—	3.68
5	0.71	1.5	1.06
6	0.80	3.0	2.40
7	0.89	4.5	4.00
8	0.97	6.0	5.82
9	1.15	7.5	8.62
	6.42		21.90

$$\text{Grand Total Displacement} = \left(\text{Total Station } \frac{0+9}{2} + \text{Total Remainder}\right) \times \text{station spacing} \times 2$$

$$= \left(\frac{(0.06+1.15)}{2} + 5.21\right) \times 1.5 \times 2$$

$$= 5.87 \times 1.5 \times 2 = 17.6 \text{ cu. ft} = 17.6 \times 64 = 750 \text{ lb}$$

$$\text{LCB} = \frac{21.90 - 3.68}{6.42} = \frac{18.22}{6.42} = 2.84 \text{ ft aft station 4 or } 8.84 \text{ ft aft station 0}$$

Centre of Gravity from Station 0

Item	Weight	Distance	Moment (Weight (lb) × Distance (ft))
Outer Sides	62.5	7.25	450
Inner Sides	84.0	6.00	504
Bottoms	77.5	7.50	580
Foredecks	7.5	0.25	2
Stem, Knee Keel	10.0	6.00	60
Aft Deck	10.0	13.00	130
Cabin Top	30.0	4.00	120
Bulkhead 1	17.5	6.00	105
Bulkhead 2	12.5	12.00	150
Bridge Deck	39.0	7.50	290
Transoms	13.8	14.00	193
	364.3		2587 lb ft

$$\text{LCG of above} = \frac{2587}{364.3} = 7.1 \text{ ft from station 0}$$

Item	Weight	Distance	Moment
Allowance of one-third	121	7.1	850
Outboard	50	12.00	600
Spars	58	5.00	290
Paraffin	20	13.00	260
Petrol	30	13.00	390
Anchor and Warp	20	13.00	260
Water	20	13.00	260
Stores	30	13.00	390
	228		2450

Three weights total = 713 lb Total Moments = 5887

$$\text{LCG} = \frac{5887}{713} = 8.2 \text{ ft aft station 0}$$

TABLE 7

Type of Stern		Canoe Stern		Transom and Flat Stern					Transom and Very Flat Stern or Chine Form				V-Chine or Stepped	
		Speed in Knots												
Length	Tons	5	6	7	8	9	10	11	12	13	14	15	16	17
20 feet	0.5	1.0	1.7	2.9	4.7	7.2	10	12	14	17	19	22		
	1.0	1.8	3.6	6.6	10.8	16	20	24	28	33	39	44		
	1.5	2.6	5.7	11	17	24	30	36	43	50	58	67		
	2.0	3.1	8.0	15	22	32	40	48	57	67	77	89		
	3.0	3.7	12	24	33	48	59	72	85	100	116	134		
25 feet	2.0	2.4	5.0	10	17	25	34	42	50	59	68	78		
	3.0	3.0	6.5	15	26	37	48	61	74	88	102	115		
	4.0	4.0	8.7	22	36	50	64	84	100	117	136	155		
	5.0	5.0	12	28	46	65	85	105	125	146	170	196		
30 feet	1.5	1.6	2.9	4.9	7.4	11	15	23	31	37	43	50	57	
	2.0	1.9	3.6	6.4	10.4	15	22	32	42	50	58	67	76	
	3.0	2.5	5.0	9.7	17	26	36	48	62	75	87	100	114	
	4.0	3.0	6.4	13	26	37	51	64	83	100	116	133	152	
	5.0	3.3	7.7	16	32	46	66	80	104	125	145	167	190	
	6.0	3.5	8.8	19	39	56	79	96	125	150	174	200	227	
	8.0	4.0	11	26	51	74	105	128	166	200	232	267	303	
40 feet	4.0	2.8	5.2	8.5	13	20	28	39	53	67	84	97	110	124
	6.0	3.5	7.0	12	20	34	50	55	89	105	126	144	164	186
	8.0	4.0	8.4	15	26	47	73	94	119	145	168	193	219	248
	10.0	4.4	9.9	18	33	61	92	122	149	180	210	242	274	310
	12.0	4.6	11	21	40	75	110	146	179	217	252	290	329	372
	14.0	5.0	12	24	46	87	128	170	208	252	294	338	384	434
	16.0	5.2	13	27	53	100	147	195	238	289	336	387	439	465
	18.0	5.6	14	30	59	112	165	219	268	325	378	435	494	558
	20.0	5.9	15	33	66	125	183	244	298	361	420	484	548	620
50 feet	8.0	4.1	7.2	13	19	28	39	55	74	99	124	150	177	205
	10.0	4.6	7.9	15	23	35	53	76	100	130	162	193	228	257
	12.0	5.0	8.8	17	27	42	66	96	122	164	199	243	283	309
	14.0	5.3	9.6	20	30	49	82	116	155	198	243	286	330	360
	16.0	5.6	10	21	34	56	98	137	183	234	278	327	376	412
	18.0	5.8	11	23	38	63	112	168	212	270	313	368	423	463
	20.0	6.0	12	25	41	70	128	192	248	300	348	408	470	515
	25.0	6.5	13	30	50	87	164	240	312	375	435	510	588	643
	30.0	7.0	14	34	57	105	197	288	374	450	522	612	705	775
	35.0	8.0	15	37	66	123	230	336	437	525	609	715	823	900

TABLE 8

Timber Scantlings

	Universal Rule	Modern Counterpart
Planking thickness	$0.16\sqrt[3]{D}$	$0.12\sqrt{D}$ if cold moulded or ply $0.15\sqrt[3]{D}$ if double diagonal
Frame heels Frame heads	$0.20\sqrt{D}$ $0.12\sqrt{D}$	$0.14\sqrt{D}$ if laminated, no taper
Deck beams	$0.20\sqrt{D}$	$0.18\sqrt{D}$ if laminated
Half beams	$0.15\sqrt{D}$	$0.13\sqrt{D}$ if laminated
Beam shelf	$0.40\sqrt{D}$	
Bilge stringer	$0.30\sqrt{D}$	
Deck planking	$0.15\sqrt[3]{D}$	$0.11\sqrt[3]{D}$ if ply

Where D is displacement in cu. ft. Apart from hull and deck planking, results are in square inches and give sectional area. Hull and deck planking results are in inches thickness. Frames and beams at 12 in. spacing.

TABLE 9

Propeller Diameters

Approximate power (from 8–150 b.h.p.) required for various r.p.m. and propeller diameters (in inches)

Diameter r.p.m.	10	11	12	13	14	15	16	17	18	19	20	21	22	23	24	25
700								8	10	12	15	20	24	30	34	40
800							8	10	13	17	20	27	33	40	50	60
900						8	10	15	18	23	30	36	45	55	65	80
1,000					8	10	14	18	24	30	40	50	60	73	88	110
1,200				9	12	17	23	30	40	53	64	80	98	125		
1,400			9	13	18	26	34	45	60	78	98	130				
1,600		9	13	18	27	38	50	65	85	120	150					
1,800	8	12	18	27	38	54	70	90	125							
2,000	10	16	24	35	50	70	96	140								
2,250	15	23	35	50	70	100	150									
2,500	18	30	45	68	96	150										
2,750	25	40	60	90	140											
3,000	33	52	80	125												

TABLE 10

Weight Calculation Summary

Total Weight	Moments Forward (about station 5)	Moments Aft (about station 5)
7522 lb = 3.36 tons	9240 lb ft	8236 lb ft

$$\text{LCG} = \frac{9240 - 8236}{7522} = 0.133 \text{ ft forward station 5 (ex ballast)}$$

LCB (from displacement calculation) = 0.808 ft aft station 5

Design displacement = 5.23 tons. Ballast weight = 5.23 − 3.36 = 1.87 tons

Distances from station 0. Stations spaced 2.33 ft

LCG of Total Weight (ex. ballast) = (5 × 2.33) − 0.133 = 11.517 ft aft station 0

Displacement acting through LCB = (5 × 2.33) + 0.808 = 12.458 ft aft station 0

Ballast = unknown, call L

Taking moments about 0

$$\begin{aligned} 5.23 \times 12.458 &= 3.86 \times 11.517 + 1.87 \times L \\ 65.2 &= 38.7 + 1.87L \\ 26.5 &= 1.87L \\ 14.2 &= L \text{ (L is 14.2 ft aft station 0)} \end{aligned}$$

TABLE 11

Lateral Plane Coefficients and Appropriate Prismatic Coefficients

Lateral Plane Coefficient (C_{LP})	0.50	0.55	0.60
Prismatic Coefficient (C_P)	0.45 to 0.475	0.48 to 0.50	0.5 to 0.515
Lateral Plane Coefficient (C_{LP})	0.65	0.70	0.75
Prismatic Coefficient (C_P)	0.51 to 0.525	0.515 to 0.53	0.52 to 0.535

TABLE 12

Keel Weight and LCG

Station	Area	S.M.	Product	Lever	Product
1	0.08	1	0.08	3	0.24
2	0.26	4	1.04	2	2.08
3	0.45	2	0.90	1	0.90
4	0.56	4	2.24	–	3.22
5	0.54	2	1.08	1	1.08
6	0.54	4	2.16	2	4.32
7	0.44	1	0.44	3	1.32
			7.94		6.72

Common interval (station spacing) = 1.44 ft   Scale 1 : 15 ($\frac{4}{5}$ in. = 1 ft)

$$\text{Multiplier} = \frac{25}{16}$$

(Square of inverted scale)

Product becomes $7.94 \times \frac{25}{16} = 12.4$

$\text{Area} = \frac{2}{3} \times 12.4 \times 1.44 = 11.9$ cu. ft   Weight $= 11.9 \times 450 = 5350$ lb

$\text{LCG} = \frac{(6.72 - 3.22)}{7.94} \times 1.44 = 0.635$ ft aft of station 4

Note:
The station numbers are those for the keel only and are not the same as those used for displacement calculation.

TABLE 13

Galvanic Series

1. Stainless Steel
2. Copper
3. Naval Brass
4. Manganese and Aluminium Bronze
5. Gunmetal
6. Cast Iron
7. Lead
8. Mild Steel
9. Aluminium Alloys
10. Galv. Mild Steel
11. Zinc

WEIGHTS, MEASURES, CONVERSIONS AND SUNDRIES

Timber

Type	Weight Lb per cu. ft	Weight Kg per cu. m	Type	Weight Lb per cu.ft	Weight Kg per cu. m
Afromosia	43	690	Oak, English	45	720
Cedar, Western Red	24	385	Pine, Pitch	44	705
Douglas Fir	33	530	Redwood, European	32	515
Elm, English	34	535	Sapele	39	625
Iroko	40	640	Spruce, sitka	28	450
Larch	35	560	Teak	41	655
Mahogany, African	33	530	Utile	41	655
Mahogany, Honduras	34	535	Yacal	62	990

Other Weights and Measures

Marine ply approx. 2.2 oz (62.5 g) per 1 mm thickness
Ferro-cement hulls under 40 ft (12 m); 11.21 lb/sq. ft (54.8 kilos/sq. m)
Ferro-cement hulls between 40 and 60 ft (12 to 18 m); 14.26 lb/sq. ft (59.5 kilos/sq. m)
Ferro-cement hulls over 60 ft (18 m); 16.65 lb/sq. ft (81.3 kilos/sq. m)
Cast iron, 450 lb/cu. ft (7200 kilos/cu. m)
Lead, 710 lb/cu. ft (11 400 kilos/cu. m)
Water, sea, 64 lb/cu. ft (1030 kilos/cu. m)
Water, fresh, 62.4 lb/cu. ft (1000 kilos/cu. m)
Water, fresh, 10 lb/gal. (1.0 kilos/litre)
Diesel fuel, approx. 8.7 lb/gal. (0.87 kilos/litre)
Petrol, approx. 7.7 lb/gal. (0.78 kilos/litre)
One gallon of a liquid occupies 0.161 cu. ft (1 litre occupies 0.001 cu. m)
Steel plate $\frac{1}{4}$ in. thick weighs 10.2 lb/sq. ft
Steel plate 6 mm thick weighs 47.0 kilos/sq. m
Aluminium alloy plate $\frac{1}{4}$ in. thick weighs 3.52 lb/sq. ft
Aluminium alloy plate 6 mm thick weighs 16.2 kilos/sq. m

Conversions

1 inch	=	0.0253 metres	1 mm	=	0.039 in.
1 foot	=	0.305 metres	1 metre	=	39.3 in. (3.28 ft)
1 sq. in	=	6.451 sq. cm	1 sq. cm	=	0.155 sq. in.
1 sq. ft	=	0.093 sq. m	1 sq. metre	=	10.76 sq. ft
1 cu. in.	=	16.386 cu. cm	1 cu. cm	=	0.061 cu. in.
1 cu. ft	=	0.028 cu. metres	1 cu. m	=	35.31 cu. ft
1 lb/ft	=	1.49 kilos/metre	1 kilo/metre	=	0.671 lb/ft
1 lb/sq. in.	=	0.070 kilos/sq. cm	1 kilo/sq. cm	=	14.22 lb/sq. in.
1 lb/sq. ft	=	4.88 kilos/sq. m	1 kilo/sq. m	=	0.204 lb/sq. in.
1 lb/cu. ft	=	16.02 kilos/cu. m	1 kilo/cu. m	=	0.062 lb/cu. ft
1 lb	=	0.454 kilos	1 kilo	=	2.205 lb

$\frac{1}{8}$ in.	=	3.17 mm;	$\frac{5}{8}$ in.	=	15.87 mm;	3 in.	=	76.19 mm;
$\frac{1}{4}$ in.	=	6.35 mm;	$\frac{3}{4}$ in.	=	19.05 mm;	6 in.	=	152.39 mm.
$\frac{3}{8}$ in.	=	9.52 mm;	$\frac{7}{8}$ in.	=	22.22 mm;			
$\frac{1}{2}$ in.	=	12.7 mm;	1 in.	=	25.4 mm;			

Index